What People Are Saying About *Make It Happen*

"*Make it Happen* is the modern bible for all things career-related for the modern professional. Everyone who wants to progress in their career and do it in a way that maintains relationships and respect with everyone around them should follow this book word for word. It's the book I wish I had early in my career."

—Brian Wong, CEO, Kiip®
Author, *The Cheat Code*

"Inside this book, D.A. Abrams shares his time-tested career development, networking, and navigational 'secrets' that he has passed down to his mentees and interns. It takes most of us a career lifetime to learn these strategies, and now we have it in the form of this handy volume. What a gift!"

—Jane Hyun, Founder & CEO
Hyun & Associates Leadership Consulting
Co-Author, *Flex*; Author, *Breaking the Bamboo Ceiling: Career Strategies for Asians*

"The 'unwritten' rules of building a career and navigating organizational politics can make or break young talent, and it's a balancing act to learn how to thrive in a multi-generational workplace. In his new book, D.A. Abrams impressively melds all of the wisdom earned over his illustrious career with his deep knowledge of young talent in organizations, and provides an invaluable how-to for those early in their careers, as they craft a personal mission that both feels authentic and exciting, and also resonates and aligns with the goals and the objectives of organizational leadership. This is a must-read for anyone, at any stage in the career journey, who wants to maximize their opportunities for growth and success."

—Jennifer Brown, President & CEO
Jennifer Brown Consulting

"D.A. Abrams captures the practical essence of what every young person entering the work force must know. Even more than that, anyone who needs a refresher on developing key relationships, as well as honing your brand, needs to read this book. What I liked most about what D.A. is doing is he puts his passion into action. The 12-Step program is smart and simple, so young people will have an instant guideline to help navigate their career. Well done, D.A.!"

—Pamela A. McElvane, CEO & Publisher,
Diversity MBA, AP&L Group Brand

"If you want a game plan to take you to the next level of success, read this book, and implement the 12 steps. D.A. has compiled numerous time-tested strategies that have propelled people in the workplace. I've personally seen people apply these strategies to elevate the impact of their efforts. Apply the advice in this book and take yourself to new levels of excellence."

—Fabian J. De Rozario, Global Talent Coach, Consultant & Trainer;
National Association of Asian American Professionals
National President & CEO, 2014-2016

"*Make it Happen* is a roadmap for successfully navigating the intersection of a purposeful life and a successful career. Regardless of what chapter of your life and career you are experiencing, there are important life lessons waiting for you in this book. Keep *Make It Happen* by your side, as the insights will help coach you through the unforeseen changes that are inevitable when you're building a career or growing a business. I just wish I had this book fifty years ago!"

—Ralph G. Moore, President
RGMA

"*Make It Happen* is an extremely insightful and well-written book. Abrams does a masterful job of helping readers rethink career and life success. This is an excellent book for everyone who cares about their future."

—Dr. Dale G. Caldwell, Author, *Intelligent Influence*
Executive Director, Rothman Institute of Innovation
and Entrepreneurship, Fairleigh Dickinson University

"If success, in whatever area you desire, is something you want, I highly recommend reading *Make It Happen*. Even as a successful entrepreneur for nearly twenty years, I still found content in the book to be helpful, inspirational, and motivational, as well as transformational. The key to success is being clear about your goals and what action you need to take in order to achieve those goals. *Make It Happen* provides great coaching on how to do just that."

—Michon Ellis, Founder and Chief Executive Officer
LimeGreen Moroch

MAKE IT HAPPEN

12 Steps to Reimagining Success and Creating the Career of Your Dreams

D.A. ABRAMS

WINGDALE HARBORS
Orlando

COPYRIGHT © 2019 D.A. ABRAMS

This work is licensed under a Creative Commons Attribution-Noncommercial-No Derivative Works 4.0 International License.

Attribution — You must attribute the work in the manner specified by the author or licensor (but not in any way that suggests that they endorse you or your use of the work).

Noncommercial — You may not use this work for commercial purposes.

No Derivative Works — You may not alter, transform, or build upon this work.

Inquiries about additional permissions should be directed to: daabrams21@gmail.com

The sole purpose of this book is to educate and inspire. There is no guarantee made by the author or the publisher that anyone following the ideas, tips, suggestions, techniques, or strategies will become successful. The author and publisher shall have neither liability nor responsibility to anyone with respect to any loss or damage caused, or alleged to be caused, directly or indirectly by the information contained in this book.

PRINT ISBN 978-1-7263-4088-5
HARDCOVER ISBN: 978-1-7334-3137-8
Published by Wingdale Harbors, Orlando Florida

To my mom, Florence P. Abrams

And to my dad, Bedford Abrams, who passed away in November 1992

ALSO BY D.A. ABRAMS

*Certified Association Executive Exam:
Strategies for Study & Success*

Diversity & Inclusion: The Big Six Formula for Success

New-School Leadership: Making a Difference in the 21st Century

*Association Management Excellence:
Become an Expert by preparing for the CAE Exam*

The Inclusion Solution: My Big Six Formula for Success

CONTENTS

FOREWORD xiii
PART 1: Lay Your Bones 1
INTRODUCTION 3
    What You'll Find Inside 6
    Why You Why Now? 8
WHAT MATTERS TO *YOU* 15
    What's a Personal Mission Statement? 17
    What Does One Look Like? 21
    Name Your Mission 26
    Value & Goals 31
    So, How Does This Make It Happen? 35
WHAT "MATTERS" TO YOUR ORGANIZATION 36
    Where Your Company Tells You What Matters 37
    What's Their Stated Purpose? 39
    Talk to Who Matters 41
    Join Up 43
    Wake-Up Call 45
WHAT'S YOUR BRAND? 46
    What Is Your Brand & Why Do You Need It? 47

    How Do I Build & Protect It? 51

    Build Your Brand but Be an Adult 56

PART 2: Stepping Up 61

STEP 1: CRACK YOUR COMPANY CULTURE 63

    What Is My Company's Culture? 66

    Why Is This Important? 76

    How Do I Dig into My Company Culture? 77

    Keep Diving Deep 81

STEP 2: MAKE YOUR BOSS LOOK GOOD 83

    First, Get to Know Your Boss 84

    Not Sure How? Try These! 88

STEP 3: WHO ARE THE COMPANY "PLAYERS"? 97

    Who's Tied to What Matters? 98

    Who's Your Keymaster? 101

    When You're Not with the Movers & Shakers 103

STEP 4: CRUSH YOUR CORE COMPETENCIES 105

    1. Develop Knowledge of Self 106

    2. Learn to Manage Up 107

    3. Manage Your Time 110

    4. Learn to Communicate Effectively 112

    5. Be Able to Present 113

    6. Be Able to Write Well 115

    7. Learn How to Sell 116

    8. Priority Setting 119

    9. Be Results Oriented 121

10. Organizational Agility 123
11. Customer Focus 124
12. Interpersonal Savvy 127
13. Diversity and Inclusion 133
14. Creative Problem Solving 137
15. Learning Agility 140
STEP 5: ADOPT A MENTOR (Or 3!) 143
    Who Are Mentors? 145
STEP 6: CULTIVATE A SPONSOR 150
    Eek! What Even *Is* a Sponsor? 151
    How to Attract Great Sponsors 153
STEP 7: TIME TO ENGAGE A COACH? 157
    What Can a Career Coach Do? 158
    Should You Look into a Coach? 160
STEP 8: ESTABLISH A GROUP OF ADVISORS 164
    Who Should I Pick? 166
    Don't Skip This Step 167
STEP 9: BE LIKABLE! 171
    Carnegie's 6 Ways to Make People Like You ... 172
    More Hacks 176
STEP 10: UNDER-PROMISE, OVER-DELIVER & ALWAYS *DO THE WORK* 180
    How to Over-Deliver and Why 182
    Take Ownership 184
    You Have to Put in the Time 185

And It Has to Be *Good!* 192
STEP 11: VOLUNTEER TO GAIN EXPERIENCE 195
    Opportunities Inside Your Organization 197
    External Opportunities 200
STEP 12: NETWORK 203
    What's the Objective? 204
    How to Hack Your Networking 210
PART 3: Pull It Together 221
CONCLUSION 223
RESOURCES 225
ACKNOWLEDGMENTS 227
ABOUT D.A. ABRAMS 229
ENDNOTES 237

FOREWORD

I AM GLAD MY FRIEND, D.A. Abrams, wrote this book. In fact, I wish I had this gem while embarking upon my own career. How you begin your work life and career is important. That's why I believe you have in your hands one of the best tools to make your path ahead a smooth one.

Making the terrifying leap from wherever you are—college, grad school, an entry-level or early-career position—into a more committed work assignment will certainly get your heart pumping. No matter how well-educated you are, how smart you are, and how proud you might be of your capabilities, it can be difficult to land with your feet firmly planted. There are a variety of reasons entering the sweet spot of your career can be tough, most of which you can't foresee from that lofty position of preparation.

Once on the ground or in your job, you move forward toward your destination (if you have one) with your own priorities. But guess what? You'll encounter others with their own sense of priorities. There are co-workers, managers, clients, and others who are all now part of your interconnected network. As you tug on the ropes of your daily efforts in one direction, they'll tug in another. Like many, you'll feel the constant pull of tension, conflict, and challenge. You soon begin to understand and accept that everyone does not have your point of view about which way to move at work, and you don't have theirs.

This inevitable contrast can be unsettling. As you look across the landscape of your work life, you might ask: Why did my manager make that decision? Why have I been assigned to this project or team? Why are others being paid more than me? How come I don't have the big office, the great account, or get to go to that conference in a cool destination? Questions you'd never imagined you'd ponder become commonplace in your mind, once you begin working inside of a living, breathing, organizational structure.

And what if you work alone? Maybe you're a part-timer, a freelancer, a salesperson, or an entrepreneur. Being in these roles can be even more challenging. Sometimes you feel alone. You might have difficulty staying motivated. There's a constant effort to remain focused. It's not always easy to bounce back from things that don't seem to go your way. You might even wish you were part of an office culture, despite the pressure. And working remotely means you can easily fall outside of the well-informed and feel you need to prove to the boss at headquarters that you're being productive.

There's more, like the challenge of learning to read between the lines in the workplace. You soon figure out there are things happening at work below the surface or behind closed doors that are not obvious. That's because you're working with people. There are confidential business strategies and plans, but sometimes there are also hidden motives, underlying agendas, and dicey corporate politics. None of this is said out loud. In other words, there's so much more that comes into play at work. And you thought it was all about having a good education!

In this timely book, *Make It Happen: Reimagining Success and Creating the Career of Your Dreams*, D. A. Abrams tells it straight. In fact, I hope you're ready. He's written this book for the large number of young people entering the workforce we call millennials. Could that be you? Between you, and me, millennials have a reputation of having difficulty with authority and constructive criticism. I know, as a Baby-Boomer, I often did. There's nothing new about that. We all must come to grips with the fact there's much more to learn than we imagined about succeeding at work and building a successful career. At first, it can be discouraging, but trust me: there's nothing better than learning early that there's another level of savvy—in fact, several levels of savvy—we can develop to propel our career forward.

According to a recent Gallup poll, 85% of workers don't like their jobs. That's an astounding statistic given that so many were excited about getting them. But something changes once we go deeper into the job. D.A. helps you decode that change and explains how you can maneuver the challenging waters ahead. D.A has provided an extraordinary framework to make your work life more gratifying and effective.

There's lots in this book on self-discovery as he walks you through how to clarify your vision and strategy and the necessary hard-nosed discussion on understanding the unwritten rules of the environment and getting results. He challenges outlooks and attitudes you may take for granted, as a member of a self-confident generation. Without undermining your confidence, he gives you a few eye-opening things to think about.

In his own career, D.A. Abrams has done a remarkable thing. He's been with the United States Tennis Association for decades—no easy feat in the tumultuous non-profit and business sectors. He's risen to become Chief Diversity Officer, a testament to his ability to work successfully with people of diverse roles and backgrounds—from the hard-driving tennis pro to the demanding corporate sponsor and the young person getting their start in the rough-and-tumble world of international sports.

Page by page, you'll discover in *Make It Happen* insights few people will share with you. The good thing is you now have D.A. to candidly spill the beans. Digest his words, put them into practice, and you'll have what it takes to *Make It Happen* for you.

André Taylor
Author, *You Can Still Win!*

André Taylor is an author and renowned thought-leader on business excellence. Learn more at www.andretaylor.com.

PART 1

Lay Your Bones

2 - MAKE IT HAPPEN

INTRODUCTION

There are opportunities everywhere, just as there have always been.

—Charles Filmore

THERE ARE MANY THINGS I enjoy about my work and professional career, including the field of tennis, which I've loved since I was a child, and the many opportunities to have impact and do great by my organization and the world through Diversity & Inclusion. But one of the aspects of my position as an executive and a leader that I find most rewarding is the opportunity to coach and mentor interns and young employees in the workplace. I am passionate about their success, encouraging of their growth, and full of ideas about how *they* can Make it Happen, whatever their chosen career path.

Because of this interest, however, and my personal commitment to the next generation of leaders, I also observe and engage with many young people who are not sure how to excel in the workplace—about how to get ahead, how to create their own success, how to turn their first or second or third jobs into careers that are satisfying and rewarding. That is why I've written *Make It Happen*. I know, from my own experience, from speaking to managers and colleagues and executives in many organizations and industries, and from my work with hundreds of interns, reports, and new employees that there *are* things you need to know, things you can do, and concrete ways to Step it Up, as I discuss in Part 2. All of these are the secret sauce for generating success where you work and for creating a career out of your job, task, or assignment.

I am sure you will find things in this book that you already know. And probably some things you're already doing. But if you're not yet making everything happen for yourself, professionally, I believe there is something in this book for you. And I can tell you this: I've worked with dozens of interns over the last twenty-five years in my job at my organization and with hundreds of young employees who are smart, hard-working, and fully capable, but *they don't know this stuff.* Not just some of these things. Not just a few of them. *Most of them don't know these 12 Steps to help themselves progress in the workplace and develop successful careers.*

I meet and work with young folk with tremendous amounts of talent, with passions and interests, even with great fundamental skills. Too often, however, they don't know what to do, exactly, to improve their work, to analyze their managers, to position themselves for raises and promotions, or even how to get done the essential tasks their bosses need accomplished.

I'm not suggesting it's easy or obvious. All the information I share in this book helped me, too, as I was coming up in my early jobs, so I hope it can be of help to any of you who are interested in learning how to move up and have the best shot at success in your work.

What You'll Find Inside

I start this book with three chapters that show how you can orient yourself to your personal mission and values, goals and objectives. Then we look at how you figure out the same things about your organization and why it's important to do so. Finally, we study how to begin looking at your own brand, which you have and continue to develop, whether you know and like it or not! These three fundamental areas of awareness will guide your choices and perspective as you work to excel in your workplace and career.

In life, you must clearly understand what you are trying to achieve. You need to identify your personal mission, your vision, and your values before you can do well in any workplace. From there, you can analyze the priorities of wherever you work—in other words, what matters to the organization. I'll show you how to do it, and I'll show you why you need to find some alignment between the two.

You may discover your company doesn't have 100% alignment with your values, but you can aspire to that. Just don't expect your company's culture and values to change once you are inside. No, if they're far apart, in order for you to be happy and successful, you will likely have to go somewhere else.

Before you begin to study and work through the Steps in Part 2, I also want you to understand your brand—your professional identity and reputation—because this whole book aims to show you how to strengthen that brand and become the person who is selected, promoted, or called upon when there is a great new opportunity, advancement, promotion, or a new move available toward success in your workplace and field. I want *you* to be the person chosen, the one who advances, when opportunity arises. And I want you to be truly ready to take advantage of those opportunities, once you get them.

Part 2 lays out all of my 12 Steps, designed for you to develop your brand and become the person your boss and team and company can count on. You want to be someone who is going to do the blocking and tackling on any challenge or project. So, through the Steps, I talk about how and why to show up on time, do what you say you're going to do, promise less, and deliver more every time. It is your charge to establish yourself in the workplace as the person who is reliable, resourceful, and prepared for opportunity.

The Steps section starts from the following truth: just being good at your job is not good enough. Of course, you *do* have to be good at your job! But to get ahead and realize your full potential, and also have a satisfying life and productive career, you'll need to understand and implement each of the 12 Steps, including the 15 core competencies I explain in Step 4.

Bottom line: if you don't grasp and get these Steps to work for you, you will find it very difficult to succeed and make things happen for you within an organization that has norms, standards, culture, levels, and opportunity. Maybe you can strike out on your own, as an entrepreneur, without mastering these Steps, but even then, you'll find many of these skills and strategies are essential to your workplace, wherever it is.

Why You Why Now?

When I began my career, the way work *worked,* for better or worse, was that our experience in the workplace began with everyone's manager putting in a lot of time at the office. He or she taught and modeled a fundamental work ethic. Company culture was baked in, so, even if you didn't know anything about your organization or your field, when you began, you had plenty of opportunities to observe. And you absolutely had to put in the time before you would be promoted or given additional responsibilities and/or a raise.

My colleague André Taylor, business-excellence advisor, Taylor Insight Worldwide, and author of *You Can Still Win!*, started his career on Wall Street. He remembers distinctly being told by the people he first worked for, "You don't know anything. You have to listen very carefully and *maybe* we'll give you an opportunity to speak and go to a meeting, but you're here to absorb."

This was humbling and it was a revelation: that there are things you don't know and you don't know you don't know them. Taylor had worked hard to be employed at his position; he was still studying constantly, and he believed he was "up on a lot of things." However, as he explains in retrospect, "I didn't understand nuance and context and politics and all those other things that surfaced. ... (I discovered) you could be right intellectually but be wrong in making a given choice (early in your job or career), because there could be a level of emphasis required that you didn't understand due to inexperience."[1]

Highly trained young biomedical engineers are thought of in the exact same way when hired today by Edwards Lifesciences. Chief Science Officer Stan Rowe CTO says, "We're not hiring you for your engineering skills because you don't really have any. What you demonstrate is engineering capability. It's really what we're investing in, right? It's a different way to look at it."[2] An employee's first years at the company involve training to apply education and knowledge to professional skills, as well as to learn and navigate Edwards' unique corporate culture.

When Taylor started his own sports company, he built it up primarily with interns and employees right out of college. Those new hires, he recalls, "all sat at my feet and my partner's, listening to our every word. They would ask constantly, 'What do we do now?' and 'How does this work?'" He finds the wide group of new and millennial employees he encounters in today's workforce, however, to be very different, culturally. "While perhaps there was a greater value attached to seasoning and age historically, today I'm not sure there is that same kind of reverence. I think that's a disadvantage for a young person, because they are in effect in an echo chamber, talking to people who are repeating the same thing."

As he puts it, "We live in a world where everything is so technologically advanced, so packaged, and so quick, there is a feeling (among many millennial workers that), because you can create the image of having arrived, you *have* arrived. And in a way that's a positive, because someone who is inspired and committed and has a contribution to make understands what that contribution is, so they can jump right in. But it takes away what can be gained from going down a path and finding that perhaps a job or direction or career is not quite right, and that you need to go down another path. The idea of making wrong turns and encountering things that unfold a bit differently than anticipated is very useful."[3]

Most likely, *you* do not see yourself or your job or learning curve the way I did, or André Taylor did for himself or his first employees, or even as Stan Rowe does with his new biomedical engineers. Millennial employees enter a workplace defined by very different technology and different management styles. It is entirely possible you are not even seeing the type of manager or boss behavior that demonstrates for you how to work, prioritize, communicate, report, network, and succeed. I see newer workers assume they can come in late, leave early, and expect life to be as quick and "right now" as their bosses and the technology around them.

But everything managers like myself learned to do, the things we absorbed and made part of our work ethic and brand, *also* must be learned and acquired and constructed by you, as well. You need to adjust your "time horizon," as André Taylor calls it, and appreciate how a career is based on a series of steps. These are things you need to learn, know, and do, even if your manager or co-workers don't teach and model them. That's why I put them together here in a clear 12-Step program.

This includes developing your writing, conversation, and listening skills. Learning how to read and communicate within your organizational culture, including making your boss's priorities your priorities. Understanding what basic abilities you need to have, practice, and develop, in order to progress and succeed. Building your brand. Being on a program of self-development. As Taylor says, "Not looking at education merely as achieving certification and being licensed to do something—also having some knowledge and depth about yourself and your field." And staying late, going the extra mile, over-delivering on your work and promises.

The core idea behind these 12 Steps is to show you the ins and outs of how you'll be able to get ahead, get your next job, get a promotion, earn more money, and develop your job into a career that inspires you.

I know you understand that you have to do a good job to excel in the workplace. But this book goes into all the other components of your professional life that will give you the best shot at a successful career. Mentoring is a big piece, for example, as you may expect. But you also need a group of advisors, maybe a coach. And, certainly, a sponsor, so someone is advocating for you in your company when you're not in the room.

You'll find this book full of tips to best prepare yourself for success.

###

WHAT MATTERS TO *YOU*

> *Your vision will become clear only when you can look into your own heart. Who looks outside, dreams; who looks inside, awakes.*
>
> —Carl Jung

YOU'VE HEARD that businesses have mission statements. Or you know that non-profit organizations are "mission-driven," their activities or programs organized around the purpose for which they came together and the social good they set out to accomplish.

When companies or associations articulate their missions, as executive coach Glenn Smith explains, their managers and leaders can then "use this statement to remind their teams why their company exists because this is what makes the company successful. The mission statement serves as a 'North Star' that keeps everyone clear on the direction of the organization."[4]

Mission statements are also part of planning and help a company's leaders envision where they want their enterprise to go, what they hope to accomplish, or what goals they should set and plan to attain in the future. Sometimes this is called the organization's "vision" or what activities a company undertakes today, in line with the mission, in order to realize concrete targets or goals in two, five, or ten years.

Well, each of us as individuals needs a mission statement, too! And it is not too soon to identify your personal mission and vision for your yourself. In fact, it's essential.

I bring this up first, even before I dive into any of my ideas for how to make happen your job and career success, because, honestly, this step defines *what* you want to make happen. And you need to know your mission before you can envision and lay out a game plan to attain your goals in the future, whatever they are—whether it's a raise, a promotion, more responsibilities, more impact, a different job, or a lifelong, successful career.

What's a Personal Mission Statement?

Carla Harper and MissionStatements.com explains what this is really succinctly: "A personal mission statement provides clarity and gives you a sense of purpose. It defines who you are and how you will live."

I invite you to understand *who you are* and *what your path is* before you do anything more. Now, this may change over time, but at any key point—say, New Year's Day or starting a job search—you want to be able to state what your values are, what you want, and what's your desired outcome. That's #1!

A noted film producer and UPM (*Dante's Peak, Collateral*), DGA Frank Capra Achievement Award winner, and former AFI associate dean, Marie Cantin, describes it this way:

"Your biggest job to begin with is to think about who you are as a person. How you like to be in the world. How you like to work with people. How you like to treat people, and how you like to be treated. You need to understand that about yourself and be honest about it, because there will be times when you have to make difficult decisions, and if you're truthful about how you like to be in the world, it will be easier to make those difficult decisions, because you won't derail and make a decision you *should* make that doesn't sit with you, rather than make the decision that is *right* with you, even if it makes other things harder...

"That's what you need to spend time thinking about: Who you are as a person and How you like to be in the world.

"(In doing this thinking), I know things about myself, like it is impossible for me to lie, so it's very hard for me to play with a poker face, because of that.

"I also figure things out really quickly and then come to a conclusion and a decision pretty swiftly. Now, *I'm* okay with that, but sometimes this puts people off because they feel I haven't spent enough time analyzing the pros and cons. But I don't work that way. I don't roll that way.

"And I like to speak from the heart and from truth. If that's not what somebody wants to hear, that's okay. I'll live with the consequences of that… But my not being able to be forthcoming about something makes it harder for me to feel like I didn't step up and do it in my authentic way. But that's a choice!"[5]

As Amelia Keiser at BrandYourself.com describes it, "A personal mission statement could be a sentence, a paragraph, or an essay that explains your purpose. The best personal mission statement examples can also be a quote or mantra that speaks to how you want to live your life. Your personal statement should change over time, but the idea is to provide a clear description of who you are and your overarching goals."[6] The point of it is to be "a guiding principle that makes it easier to say no to things that don't support it and helps you to focus your time and energy on the things that truly matter to you."

So, before writing your mission statement, take some time to think about how you operate, how you feel best, what you respond to well and poorly, and, most important, what really matters to you. This should be thinking on all levels, because this is your life! So, it's about your politics and your tastes, your strongest times of day, and the ways you learn and work best. It's about what arenas really excite you—Sports? Arts? Finance? Sales? And if sports, what sports? If management, what aspects of it?

As for myself, I was a teen tennis player and loved the sport growing up—I liked the strategy, the culture, the environment, the ups and downs, the challenges it brought, and the lessons it taught me. So I was, and continue to be, very excited and inspired to work for my organization.

As I grew in the USTA, I discovered the power and impact of Diversity & Inclusion. It resonates with my mission, with the kind of change I want to bring forth in the world, and I know intimately how much success it can bring to any company or association. I really appreciate how everyone wins through D & I; it really connects with my personal story, so I remain committed to work in this field, doing this type of job.

What's your story?

As Marie Cantin reminds us, "In any human enterprise, it's not just the end product that matters. It's how you get there. That's why ... checking in with who you are and how you like to be in the world is really important, because that can be a guiding principle that will lead you through minefields of decision-making that would otherwise be paralyzing and not lead you anyplace productive. Different people navigate differently, based on their pain threshold for operating a certain way. I don't have a value judgement on that. There are just things I can't do that other people can do. It's great! They should do it. But I can't."[7]

What are your pain points? What are your strengths?

Who are you?

What Does One Look Like?

Amelia Keiser at BrandYourself.com assembled some of her company's favorite personal mission statements, from people in a variety of fields, from media to tech and beyond.[8] Read a few and see what you think!

Media mogul and OWN CEO Oprah Winfrey: "To be a teacher. And to be known for inspiring my students to be more than they thought they could be."

Tesla and SpaceX CEO and lead designer/product architect Elon Musk: "If something's important enough, you should try. Even if the probable outcome is failure."

Nobel Prize laureate, student, and young women's rights activist Malala Yousafzai: "I want to serve the people. And I want every girl, every child to be educated."

Chinese Artist Ai Weiwei: "It's not about the work, it's about saying something."

Here are a few more, to keep you brainstorming before you sit to pen your own:

Inline skating instructor Liz Miller: "I am a committed recreational skater's advocate. I will do everything in my power to ensure that novices achieve the most positive first experience possible. This means encouraging them to buy the best equipment they can afford and to learn the basic skills, especially how to use the heel brake. To fight skate bans due to congested popular trails, I will help more experienced skaters build their speed and hill skills, so they can train on a wider variety of trails without the risk of alienating other users. I will continue to encourage all skaters to improve their skills so they can adopt a well-rounded inline lifestyle."

Latin pop star Soraya is "on a mission to educate women about breast cancer, hoping to inspire women to take control of their own breast health, by sharing her personal survival experience and life-saving message." After surviving breast cancer herself, she now collaborates with the Susan B. Komen Foundation, Living Beyond Breast Cancer, and others to realize her vision of educating women all over the world about breast cancer.

Maybe your mission will be lofty or maybe it's pretty down-to-earth. Maybe it's short, maybe it includes three to five personal values, or maybe it looks at a wider set of life facets and attitudes. That's up to you.

Here is another, more personal example:

"To be a decent person who is respected by family, friends, loved ones, and my chosen communities. I am here to make a positive difference despite being imperfect. My work reflects my values and enables me to travel widely and enhance the lives of others. People will remember me for being there to lend a hand, keeping an open mind, and for getting involved in issues that matter most to me."[9]

Or: "My mission is to act as an instrument of positive change in my family, my work, and my community. I will utilize all of the talents that God has given me and will participate in all aspects of my life with energy, purpose and gratitude. I will utilize my talents in strategy and administration to ensure that my home is loving and calm, my workplace is productive and positive and my community is responsive and growing. Through this focus I will give more than I take and will provide a positive role model for my children."[10]

Maybe yours will be really focused on work and career, like this one: "My mission is to create and lead a dream team where everyone is playing to their strengths." Or "My mission is to help project managers transform into impactful project leaders."[11] Or perhaps you'll gravitate to one that's more general and visionary, aspirational, like DailyWorth.com founder Amanda Steinberg's personal mission statement: "To use my gifts of intelligence, charisma, and serial optimism to cultivate the self-worth and net-worth of women around the world."[12]

You can also follow the lead of these top CEOs, whose missions are a combination of the personal and professional[13]:

Denise Morrison, Campbell Soup Company—"To serve as a leader, live a balanced life, and apply ethical principles to make a significant difference."

Richard Branson, The Virgin Group—"To have fun in (my) journey through life and learn from (my) mistakes."

Katie Arnold, *Talk Less, Say More* blog—"To constantly be striving to be the best version of myself—in my job, with my health and fitness, with my relationships with family and friends, and with my emotional well-being."

Amy Ziari, Bateman Group—"To live life with integrity and empathy, and be a positive force in the lives of others."

It's not about being any one way. It's about setting aside the time to develop a personal mission that suits *you*, and then checking back in with your unique statement when you have choices, questions, or decisions, and as you set out your goals for the upcoming year.

Name Your Mission

After you ask yourself lots of questions and think through what you love and hate, as well as how you thrive (and *don't*), you'll be ready to write your own great mission statement.

Now, as Stephen Covey, author of *The 7 Habits of Highly Successful People,* reminds us, "A mission statement is not something you write overnight... But, fundamentally, your mission statement becomes your constitution, the solid expression of your vision and values. It becomes the criterion by which you measure everything else in your life," and is about "defining the personal, moral, and ethical guidelines within which you can most happily express and fulfill yourself."[14]

Amelia Keiser from BrandYourself.com suggests these steps to get you started[15]:

1) **Schedule some quiet time to just write.** In order to crack this nut and get your statement written, set aside a few minutes each day for a week or two. Maybe it's five minutes and maybe it's thirty; maybe first thing in the morning or right before bed. Just set an appointment with yourself and let yourself drop in to do this special project.

2) **Start with a question, a new one or two every day.** You can lead with a big one that might inspire a big list from you, like, "What's important to me?" You can try thinking deep, looking back at what you hope to accomplish, and ask, "What do I want my legacy to be?" But try a few practical ones, too, like, "What does my ideal day look like?" or "When do I feel most calm?" How about "feel most powerful?"

Consider questions about your nature, your strengths and weaknesses, like, "What makes me different from other people?", "What am I great at?" and "When do I feel most useful?", "What makes me feel alive?" and "What am I most proud of?"

And also look ahead and dream by asking things like, "What do I wish I made more time to do?", "What's something I haven't done that I want to do before I die?" and "If I had an extra hour each day, how would I fill it?"

The whole idea is to think about who you are, who you *want* to be, and, like Marie Cantin described, what you are willing to do to get there. The more specific you can be about things you've done or avoided, succeeded or failed at, the easier it will be to extrapolate your mission from your meditations.

3) **Determine a purpose.** I really like this idea from Barrie Davenport at her *Live Bold and Bloom* blog. She suggests you write down a purpose for the four fundamental elements of who you are:

> - Physical
> - Mental
> - Emotional
> - Spiritual

In each of these areas, ask yourself, "What is the most important way I want to express myself?"

She says, "See yourself as CEO of each of these four areas. As CEO of your physical life, your purpose might be to *treat your body as sacred* by practicing fitness, healthy eating, daily affection, and pleasurable physical experiences. Your purpose for your mental life might be *to become a lifelong learner* by expanding your skills, problem-solving, and challenging yourself."[16]

4) **Review your entries**. Once you can put the pen down and sit back to look everything over, do you see different sorts of patterns emerge? What would you say comes through as your top goal or goals? Can you link that up to your greater purpose?

Thinking about your personal life, your professional life, and your interests and passions, start to sketch out a list of your life's priorities. You can also name a top priority for who you are physically, mentally, emotionally, and spiritually—whatever works for you.

5) **Make a statement.** After reviewing all your work, you can start to pull together your own unique Mission Statement. Keiser quotes the author William Arruda (*Career Distinction; Ditch, Dare, Do*) for a cool way to consider your mission. Think of it as:

"The value you create + who you're creating it for + the expected outcome."

With this formula, you can incorporate your strengths and value along with how you intend to use those talents.

6) **Hung up on identifying "the value you create" part? Try asking around.** You can absolutely ask friends and colleagues who know you well to help you figure this one out! And it's great to canvas people who know you in different ways or who see you in various capacities. Try asking them, "Hey, what do I do great?"

7) **Look to your idols.** It really helps to take inspiration from inspiring people. Maybe it's famous people; maybe it's books on growth and success; maybe it's parents or teachers or mentors who live life the way

you aspire to. They can all contribute to your questions or your answers. And a lot of them have their own personal Mission Statements!

###

Finally, after all your hard work, don't let that Mission Statement be a stranger. Keep it around. Check in with it at your desk or in your journal. Maybe even use parts of it on your webpage or LinkedIn profile.

At the very least, as Barrie Davenport adds, "Review the personal mission statement regularly and feel free to revise and update it as you continue to ponder your values and goals. Keep it within view, so you can read it regularly. Use it as your personal framework for your life, and every time you make an important decision, let your mission statement be your guide."[17]

Value & Goals

Before you can truly dive into a job, career, or project, part of your process of identifying and understanding exactly where you want to be involves **identifying your values.** You can see these as that little list you did in number 4, above, writing down a purpose for the four fundamental elements of who you are:

> ➢ Physical
>
> ➢ Mental
>
> ➢ Emotional
>
> ➢ Spiritual

These create an ideal springboard for setting monthly, annual, and long-term goals. So, for me, I check in on the things I value at the start of each new year. And the five things I value generally remain the same, year to year. My personal values are:

1. Lifelong learning
2. Family & friends
3. Health & wellness
4. Financial freedom
5. Spirituality (not religion)

What are yours? Can you do a list, now that you've thought through your Mission Statement?

This isn't a static "item" as part of your identity, though, even if your values don't change from year to year. What I do in my annual review is write up a single page on which I review my values and identify what I'm trying to achieve in each of those five areas in the year ahead. Then, I brainstorm on ways to attain them or get there.

I add metrics wherever I can, because that gives me benchmarks and concrete ways to review and adjust how and what I'm doing. So, say, around health and wellness, I aspire to work out fifteen times a month. When I get to the thirtieth, I can ask, how'd I do? When I set a goal for eating better, maybe jot down some ideas for the year or month—more veggies? Meat only 3 times a week?—then I weigh myself each day I'm in town. These seem like little things, but they become proactive and concrete activities that help me stay on course. They're also doable, but they really make a difference in my life plan and outlook. This strategy can help you stay on course, too, so you live up to what you want to be.

I also use these goals and strategies I enumerate on New Year's to guide me throughout the next year. I do a check-in every month and review how I'm doing. I may tweak or expand the specifics around my goals and achievements or I might just stay the course, if I'm doing well. I even talk about some of this process and progress with my advisors and mentors, as I'll discuss later, in the 12 Steps section, Part II.

In line with my strategy, *Forbes* writer Patrick Hull takes out his personal mission statement in the New Year, too, and crafts a set of goals. He has these three keys to turning this into an effective an inspiring exercise:

1. "Include specific and attainable goals. Don't be vague and aim for something you're unlikely to reach, which will set you up for failure.

2. "Outline how you plan to achieve those goals. Just listing your goals is only half the battle. You must consider how you will get there.

3. "Hold yourself accountable by asking a mentor, business partner, or a trusted advisor to meet with you quarterly to discuss the progress on your personal goals and mission statement."[18]

So, How Does This Make It Happen?

Well, we're getting to that. I promise! But you're going to find that your Personal Mission Statement, your values, and your goals, what you're trying to accomplish this year and in the next five years, are the very best guides to finding jobs or for succeeding in professional opportunities at companies that best match what's important to you. Ideally, you want to know what's important to you before you get or change jobs, so you can find a company/organization that will afford you a good work experience. In addition, doing this work may motivate you to leave the one you're in and find a better fit. Because this stuff is bedrock.

Next, we look at **what your company wants**. Yes. You need to figure that out, too, in order to make anything happen.

###

WHAT "MATTERS" TO YOUR ORGANIZATION

"Don't play games that you don't understand, even if you see lots of other people making money from them."

—Tony Hsieh, CEO of Zappos

BEFORE YOU CAN make your job great, build your career, and ensure things happen in your workplace, you need to figure out what "matters" to your company, association, organization, and employer, just as you figured out what matters to you.

This awareness and understanding is going to come into play in a lot of ways, as you'll see in the 12 Steps, but I say it here because, oddly enough, a lot of young employees *do not figure this out in time.* They are often good researchers in advance of interviews; they are certainly smart and generally strong workers. But you need to take this extra step of drilling down on what is important to your particular company or organization in order to succeed and get ahead.

And it's not obvious, in some ways. So, let's look at where you can find this out.

Where Your Company Tells You What Matters

There is public information put out by any company, association, or entity you work for. Some of it is their public face; some of it is in the public record. This is not *all* you need to know, but it's a great start. And if you don't know what's there, you will always be doing your job at a disadvantage.

Of course, start with your company's website. This is how they put themselves forward, their in-depth billboard. It is full of information that can really help you, even if it's about products or services or topics that aren't directly related to your job.

What you will see there, first of all, is the obvious and visual. Your company logo, colors, style, font. The sort of human and graphic images they showcase. The feel of the place. The titling and messages they highlight. What do they say to you?

Then consider how they describe themselves, what their programs and policies are, where and when they operate. And how about the *why*? Do they have their own mission statement, vision, and goals stated somewhere? (We'll talk about how your organization expresses that or lives up to it a little later, but what they put right up front is valuable for your analysis. A lot of companies are very committed to living their values and realizing their mission, so that can guide and inform a lot of what is expected of you.)

The financial information is also really interesting. Some companies post their annual report and even their audits on their websites somewhere. What did they gross? What did they accomplish? What are their targets for the next years? For a non-profit or exempt organization, you also want to look at any 990s made available. If they aren't part of a website, check them out at Guidestar.com.

Websites are also a great start to figuring out who the company decision-makers are. Who is who? Who is featured or important? How is your organization *organized*, with wide management or lots of vertical departments?

Then there is the material they give to you, specifically, as a new or recent employee: a company handbook, and employee manual, an onboarding packet, video, training or welcoming sessions. Review and listen to these carefully about the institutional priorities and policies they communicate to you.

What's Their Stated Purpose?

Maybe it's on the website. Maybe it's the company handbook or employee onboarding materials. But most every organization, big or small, has a mission statement. After your online research, can you answer these questions from Patrick Hull of Bizilla, in *Forbes?*[19]:

1. What do we do?

2. How do we do it?

3. Whom do we do it for?

4. What value are we bringing?

If you're working for a smaller company or entrepreneur, maybe the corporate mission statement is more concise—it needs to be specific, "so your customers understand your purpose and how you provide value to them."

As Hull reminds us, your company's mission statement is going to tell you "what the company does for its customers," but it's also for you, as an employee, to keep you "focused on their objectives."

If you can't find a stated mission, can you piece together or identify what *Fast Company* defines as your organizational goals? These are "strategic objectives that a company's management establishes to outline expected outcomes and guide employees' efforts."[20] You want to piece together what principles your company uses to plan for the future and to evaluate what they've accomplished, as well as to motivate and inspire employees—that's you!

Why is this helpful? Well, "Organizational goals inform employees where the organization is going and how it plans to get there. When employees need to make difficult decisions, they can refer to the organization's goals for guidance.

"Goals promote planning to determine how goals will be achieved. Employees often set goals in order to satisfy a need; thus, goals can be motivational and increase performance."[21]

Your organization is supposed to make sure you know all this, so you know what you need to accomplish, both today and looking forward. But managers may not do this well enough for you, or soon enough. So, for your own well-being and success, consider taking this on, yourself. It will become much easier for you to succeed and do your job great, if you identify how your work contributes to what matters to your particular company or association.

See if you can ascertain all of that, after your research. Now, how do you feel about it? Are you on board to help make that happen for your bosses and your organization?

Talk to Who Matters

Continue your exploration of what matters to your particular organization, because you're not going to get

100% of what you need to know from just what's out there in public or in print. And when you start drilling down, you may begin to fill in some gaps, find some more pieces of critical information, and even find some key inconsistencies that can be important to your chances for success.

I encourage you to interview or sit down and have coffee with as many of your company's decision-makers as you can. See how high up the corporate ladder you can climb for ten minutes, to sit with key executives. See how many different departments you can visit, to learn a little more about who runs them and what they do.

Don't be nervous. It's not an imposition, as some of you may think. It shows terrific initiative along with a healthy respect and curiosity about your organization and its success. Even if you're an intern, use your time to meet with people and understand what they do and how that fits into the company overall. (And, side benefit: these folks get a little introduction to *you*, at the same time. We'll talk later about how and why you want to get noticed, in order to make things happen for yourself.)

As you do this, especially if it's early in your time at an organization, start to get a sense of what's what. When you read or hear something once or for the first time about your company or its policies, you may not know yet if it's true or not. But if you can talk to enough people and hear similar sorts of things, that is very validating. And having details and information and understanding is going to be really helpful for you.

Join Up

Later, I'll talk more about how joining your organization's Affinity Groups or your company's Employee Resource Groups (ERGs) or Business Resource Groups can help you in various ways, and in different ways, maybe, than you expect. But for now, one of the first things you can do to expand your awareness of your own company and who's doing what is to join up and take advantage of what these groups have to offer you.

There is probably some socializing, for starters, which is a nice way to get to know people in your company whom you may not run into every day. There are also invariably networking and information-gathering opportunities, where you can learn about your company and your field, plus maybe the competitors or maybe things coming up in different departments other than yours.

But the best part about these groups, in terms of how you can make things happen, is they are really great ways to figure out what matters to your organization. They often provide you access to top management. Sometimes, they are aligned or charged with specific company priorities or tasks, so you can see first-hand what your organization is trying to accomplish.

Also, by participating in these Resource Groups, you can develop leadership skills. You can show and tell about your own strengths and information. You can even get involved in cross-functional teams through these ERGs, where you get to learn to do things not directly part of your training or job function.

Most every company, association, or organization has a variety of these groups, but I notice oftentimes newer employees or younger members of the workforce don't join right away. Give it a try! If only to complete your analysis of what matters to your own company. They can really be the secret sauce!

Wake-Up Call

Are you working at the right place? It's good for you to know this, before you put all your efforts into studying and implementing the 12 Steps I'm about to share with you.

Because, if your mission and vision and essential *"who you are"* and *"what you want"* are really very different than your organization's mission and values, you are going to be very uncomfortable and have a hard time attaining success.

You can't get what you want at a place that doesn't want the same thing.

You won't reach out to the right mentors or attract the best sponsors, if you (and they) don't know who you are and what you want to accomplish. You can't figure out how to advance in a place if it's the wrong place for you.

Make sense? Do you fit? Are you in the best place to learn and apply your talents?

###

WHAT'S YOUR BRAND?

"Your work is going to fill a large part of your life, and the only way to be truly satisfied is to do what you believe is great work. And the only way to do great work is to love what you do."

—Steve Jobs, co-founder, Chairman, CEO of Apple Inc.

IT USED TO BE we used our early jobs, projects, successes, raises, and maybe speeches or publicity about our work to build our "brand." Millennials now come to the workplace already acutely aware of branding, both their own and other people's.

Part of that, of course, comes from growing up with social media. As Facebook founder Mark Zuckerberg succinctly observes, "Think about what people are doing on Facebook today. They're keeping up with their friends and family, but they're also building an image and identity for themselves, which in a sense is their brand."

After all this thinking about mission statement and purpose and vision and goals, do you really need to worry about your brand, too?

Absolutely. It is *you*! Through social media, you've already begun to establish your brand. Now it becomes what you are defining and refining and building through your work and decisions. That will always be true, but especially so in your first few jobs out of college and in the workforce. Plus, it's going to have a direct correlation to your success and happiness in making things happen.

To connect right back to what we covered in the first chapter, as Vayner Media CEO Gary Vaynerchuk puts it, "You have to understand your own personal DNA. Don't do things because I do them or Steve Jobs or Mark Cuban tried it. You need to know your personal brand and stay true to it."

What Is Your Brand & Why Do You Need It?

As the editors at BrandYourself.com remind you, "Whether you own a company, just graduated college, or are simply looking for a job, you have to craft a brand that makes sense to you and the audience you want to influence.

"Assume that everyone you care about impressing will look you up online, because, statistically speaking, that's pretty darn accurate"[22]

They conducted a Harris Interactive Study subtitled, "How our personal search results affect our everyday relationships, from who we do business with, who we vote for, and even who we date." The key findings that impact you, in your new jobs or early career, won't surprise you at all:

> ➤ "Almost all online U.S. adults use search engines to look up other people. 86% used a search engine like Google to find more information about another person.

> ➤ But most people aren't well represented: 75% of online U.S. adults have searched their own name, yet almost half (48%) say most of the search results about them aren't positive, and nearly a third (30%) say nothing shows up at all.

> Among U.S. adults who have searched someone online, nearly half (42%) have searched someone before doing business with them, and 45% have found something that made them decide NOT to do business."[23]

So, how does this relate to you, other than you fully expect to Google anyone you work with and be Googled by everyone you meet?

Well, as Tim Ferriss *(The 4-Hour Workweek)* puts it, "Personal branding is about managing your name—even if you don't own a business—in a world of misinformation, disinformation, and semi-permanent Google records. Going on a date? Chances are that your 'blind' date has Googled your name. Going to a job interview? Ditto."

Being aware that you have a brand, identifying what it is, and then working to build, maintain, and stay consistent with it is what you need to be thinking about.

Gary Vaynerchuk adds, "It's important to build a personal brand because it's the only thing you're going to have. Your reputation is online, which in the new business world is pretty much the game, so you've got to be a good person. You can't hide anything, and, more importantly, you've got to be out there at some level."

Skidmore College made national news this spring when a 2010 graduate, now an NPR producer, went back to profile their very popular course, "Presenting the Brand Called Me," taught by Dean Paul Calhoun.[24] In this undergraduate class, students learn though practice "to present themselves in a variety of situations related to career development ... (and such) contexts (as) formal job and information interviews, formal and short impromptu presentations, and dialogues regarding career issues." By the end of the semester, each student leaves with "their own elevator pitch, a short story about themselves guaranteed to make a lasting impression in any professional scenario."

It helped them all get jobs and internships, which you likely have already done, as this is pre-professional and preparatory work. Did you recognize how you were presenting your nascent brand in job interviews or pitching yourself for a project?

Now that you're out in the world, in your jobs, you want to build your success through knowing your brand and leveraging it with the 12 Steps, starting with the next chapter.

How Do I Build & Protect It?

To build and develop your own great brand, digital marketing expert Krista Neher (*Social Media Field Guide*) suggests, "Start by knowing what you want and who you are, build credibility around it, and deliver it online in a compelling way."

Think of "your brand (as) a gateway to your true work. You know you are here to do something—to create something or help others in some way. The question is, how can you set up your life and work so that you can do it? The answer lies in your brand. When you create a compelling brand, you attract people who want the promise of your brand–which you deliver." (Dave Buck, leadership coach and CEO, CoachVille.)

In their book *The Road to Recognition*, Barry Feldman and Seth Price remind you to first **Decide that you are brand worthy.** They quote the actor Kevin Hart (*Ride Along*), who says, "Knowing your self-worth is extremely important, people. I own my brand, I make smart decisions for my brand, I protect my brand."

Yes, that's easy for a movie star to say, right? Or it's really obvious with brand vanguards and ambassadors like Kim Kardashian or Stephen Curry or Gigi Hadid, who sometimes seem like nothing *but* a brand. But your own brand is important, too. It gives you "a code to live up to; you stand for something." So, "What is that something that you want people to think of when they hear your name?"[25]

Start with how you want to be perceived. What do you want people to think about you? This is the beginning of being "strategic about personal branding."

As Lisa Gansky (*The Mesh: Why the Future of Business is Sharing*) writes, "Your brand is your public identity, what you're trusted for. And for your brand to endure, it has to be tested, redefined, managed, and expanded as markets evolve. Brands either learn or disappear."

And just like a company's brand is a sacred promise, "personal branding is the art of becoming knowable, likable, and trustable." That's how John Jantsch of *Duct Tape Marketing* puts it.

Because of the prominence of our digital landscape and social media profiles, you likely already know how easy it is to begin creating an online brand. In fact, you were probably warned about it by college admissions counsellors (Scrub that Facebook page, right? Watch those hard-partying Insta posts…) or in career development classes like at Skidmore.

According to a 2016 study done by Career Builder, the key personal content that could now affect how you're evaluated by an HR department, company, or organization's decision on whether or not to hire someone includes:[26]

- ❖ "Provocative or inappropriate photographs, videos or information – 46%
- ❖ "Information about candidate drinking or using drugs – 43%
- ❖ "Discriminatory comments related to race, religion, gender, etc. – 33%
- ❖ "Candidate bad-mouthed previous company or fellow employee – 31%
- ❖ "Poor communication skills – 29%"

This ease and access and opportunity to share and promote yourself through social media, blog posts, and personal websites today "is great for those looking to build out their positive brand for others to find." But, as BrandYourself.com also reminds you, "Anything you say or do in front of an audience (live, as well as on the Internet) becomes a part of your brand and what you stand for. In addition, a lack of an online presence can also hinder whatever opportunities you are seeking."[27]

In her Online Reputation Guide for college students, Katie Smith reiterates, "more and more employers and graduate schools are using Google search results as a benchmark to determine whether or not certain candidates meet their criteria. In fact, 75% of HR departments are required to research a candidate online before making a hire."[28]... Your social presence online can directly impact how an employer evaluates you as a job candidate.

"According to a study conducted by JobVite.com, 92% of companies use social media for recruiting, and 45% of Fortune 500 firms include links to social media on their career page sections. ... The fact is employers are using the

Internet to make sure candidates have reputations that can adequately represent and speak for the reputation of the company. All the more reason for making sure that the web results you control are as clean as they can be … (starting with) social media."[29]

As you begin to construct your own "elevator pitch" and your own holistic understanding of what your brand is, follow the advice of Amelia Keiser for starting to build your brand and first "audit everything that's already out there. Scan your search results in Google, and really review what pictures, videos, posts, comments, etc. are out there about you on social media. Take stock of all this and pay close attention to content that is damaging, irrelevant or personal … things probably not in line with your overall goals … Clean up the content that doesn't fit the professional image you're trying to project.

"Once you've cleaned everything up, work on a regular strategy to consistently publish high-quality posts, and engage with your growing network."[30]

Use your content postings and social media to develop, support, and augment your brand, remaining consistent with your mission. Do a regular check-in to ensure that it adds up to the brand you've devised for yourself. You can still post family photos or great adventures shots! Just stay positive and consistent, so they enhance your image, your brand, and they communicate true things about who you are and what you're here to do.

Build Your Brand but Be an Adult

We're talking about mission and brand here, before I dive into my 12 Steps, because they're important and foundational. But just as important to remember is that you are relatively early in what will be a long and interesting career. Like your vision and goals, your career may change or even veer off in a wildly different direction. But it is always an evolution, a process, and this is near the beginning!

So, think of your brand as something you are building and promoting through these first jobs, not something you are locked into and walk in with. In the same way as your mission will become richer and stronger as you undertake these ideas for success, so will your brand become more potent over time. Allow it to grow; don't dig in your heels on it just yet.

And as *The Muse* editor, Alyse Kalish, reminds us so aptly: it never hurts to check in, as you live your mission and promote your brand, that you're a responsible and mature adult in the workplace. There are guidelines and expectations, what she calls "The 9 Rules." When you forget them, you can do real, swift damage to your brand and reputation, even lose your job.

So, to close out this section on knowing who you are, what you're about, and where you're working, before you launch into all the great ideas for how to grow your career and make things happen, let's revisit her 9 Rules. As she says, "these may sound basic, but take note—immature moves could change the way people perceive you, and determine whether you actually succeed in your career (or come out looking like an uncontrollable child)."[31]

1. **"Show Up on Time:** Be on time in the morning to meetings, to presentations, to company all-hands, to off-sites—or early, if possible. And, speaking of time, stay late when it's needed or expected of you.

2. **Dress Appropriately:** You know what this means in your office.

3. **Do What's Asked:** Your boss gives you an assignment or asks you to chip in on something or wants you to attend a meeting, do it and do it well—because they asked, and because not doing it (or doing it poorly) will only hurt you in the long run.

4. **Respect Your Co-workers:** Be kind, honest, and patient with them. Along those same lines, avoid gossip and respect your co-working space, too (including those dirty dishes!). Make sure you're cultivating good relationships with everyone you meet (even if it's just a professional relationship).

5. **Keep Your Complaining Quiet:** There will be times when you'll have to do work that you don't enjoy, feels tedious, or takes an excessive amount of your time and energy. Real adults take these moments in stride. They may not enjoy them, but they don't whine to anyone who'll listen.

6. **Keep an Open Mind:** Your career, for better or worse, will never be truly stagnant. People will

change, your job will change, your company will change, your interests will change. So, be open to new possibilities, whether it's a new assignment, a new networking opportunity, or a new person to get to know. Let people and things surprise you—and if they don't, be okay with moving on to something else.

7. **Be Resilient:** Change, mishaps, failure—they all make you a stronger, wiser, more exciting person. When they happen, don't let them get you down. Adults know they have to own their career to thrive in it, even if that means failing over and over again. Practice being resilient in everything you do, and people will never doubt your maturity and potential.

8. **Practice Self-Awareness:** Know when you're frustrating others or not pulling your weight. (We'll talk about this in my 12 Steps, too.) Know when you're wrong and when you can do better. When you're aware you're doing something right, take note of that, too!

9. **Get Comfortable with Confrontation:** Conflict and confrontation at work are inevitable. ... You'll have to face doing difficult things. Rather than avoid these situations, be an adult and accept them. Learn how to give tough feedback (and receive it). This will only make you a more respected and confident leader."[32]

With these basics in mind for leading with a solid brand and purpose, let's look at how you can step up to grow your career and really make it happen.

###

PART 2

Stepping Up

62 - MAKE IT HAPPEN

STEP 1

CRACK YOUR COMPANY CULTURE

> *"If you can dream it, you can do it."*
>
> —Walt Disney, founder, the Disney Brothers Cartoon Studio, Disneyland

WE HAVE A SET of things that matter to the success of the organization where I work, the USTA. These are the things we are talking about all the time in my professional environment. In my case, this means, of course, the U.S. Open, our biggest and most well-known program (as well as our chief income source). And now we are also very invested in our new youth brand, Net Generation.

In everything my organization says or does—internally, like in budgeting or planning or hiring, and externally, in marketing and appearances and events—you would clearly see how these two things are *very* important to us.

As we discussed in the second chapter, while what matters to your organization may not be hard to figure out, you do need to know what it is, in order to become successful where you work. It may not be clear in all the PR, but you can discover what matters most through various public reports and on the website, and you can analyze where your company is spending its money. Again, it doesn't necessarily matter what your company says publicly. Oftentimes that may align with what you learn is important, but not always. In order to do well in a company, however, *figure out what matters.*

Now you're ready to figure out your **company culture.** The culture is how things are done around your organization. *Really* done. So, for example, if you have studied how your company spends its money and time, if they *say* Diversity or Inclusion are really important to them, for example, but you do not find much of that happening—in outreach, in programs, in hiring, in resource groups, in scorecards or reports—that is something to notice.

If, for another example, your boss says, "I really want dissenting opinions," yet people don't express them in the meetings and reports and situations you observe, there's a reason why. *Why*? He or she doesn't *really* want that! And nor do the people under them!

Every company has different ways of getting things done, of sharing information, of bringing the boss or top managers to a decision or an action-step or a clarification. In some places, you can get questions answered fastest from a top boss or manager by putting it through their assistant and having him or her ask for you, when the boss has a break. In other places, you need to write a memo or make an appointment and go in with a tight list of what you need to ask. In other places, you need to pipe up strategically in pre-scheduled meetings for project staff or departments. Sometimes these are good forums for information and instruction but not dissent; at other companies, these are the places to object, to register concern, or to spitball wildly different ideas or directions. Either way, you need to learn this stuff!

What Is My Company's Culture?

You can think of your company culture as the organization's personality. As such, as Alison Doyle explains at The Balance Careers, it is going to define the environment where you work.

"Company culture includes a variety of elements, including work environment, company mission, value, ethics, expectations, and goals. For example, some companies have a team-based culture, with employee participation on all levels, while others have a more traditional and formal management style. Other companies have a casual workplace without many rules and regulations."[33]

You're likely going to do some observation, some research, and some investigation to define your own organization's unique and particular culture. Some companies, like Google, an organization with a really distinct corporate culture, are very public about it. They let it be known and are very publicly proud about how it "…still feels like a small company with an informal atmosphere, even though it has grown tremendously ... At lunchtime, almost everyone eats in the office café, sitting at whatever table has an opening and enjoying conversations with Googlers from different teams... Every employee is a hands-on contributor... no one hesitates to pose questions directly to Larry or Sergey in our weekly all-hands ("TGIF") meetings *(later moved to Monday, since people liked them so much—Ed.)*–or spike a volleyball across the net at a corporate officer."

Google is an interesting case to look at because they help an employee understand their corporate priorities through what they do, as a company. For example, they want to be sure you have no distractions from doing good and copious work, if you are an employee. So, they have lots of perks, like haircuts and car washes, gyms and meals, which means you don't have to leave their campus to take care of daily stuff. In other words, their company culture is "to take care of you while you take care of work."[34]

Also, they're an analytics company—that's clear; that's the mission! But it is their *culture* to apply analytics to creating their culture, as well. For example, they happen to know "the optimal lunch line at the cafeteria is three to four minutes. Longer than that and they're wasting time; shorter than that and they don't get to meet anyone new."[35] Guess how long you can expect to wait for lunch, if you work there!

Google is a place where you can work in whatever way you want: maybe you work best at a desk, decorated with personal items; maybe you're better, faster, and more creative in a beanbag chair or on a swing set—this is a company that happens to let you work wherever.[36]

Yours might, too. *But they might NOT.* Your company culture investigation will let you discover these things concretely, so you can act.

The key is to explore and understand this part of your company right up top, as soon as possible. As *Harvard Business Review* reports, "When you join an organization, you have a short window of time to adapt to its culture. It's the old 90-day rule. And we know too many talented individuals who have stumbled in their new company because they failed to read the cultural tea leaves. This happens because most organizations don't explain the cultural rules to newcomers, and new hires are so focused on the job and the new boss that they overlook the rules' profound influence. Yet understanding them plays a big role in your initial success. Being cognizant of not just what your colleagues do but how they work matters if you want to be effective and be perceived well."[37]

They mention five key aspects of organizational culture where you need to focus, so you'll start navigating your workplace and excelling in your job. Let me explore four of them for you to consider. (And hey, even if you're reading this after being at your company 90 days, no reason not to give these a try right away! It's never too late to crack your corporate codes!)

1. **Relationships:** As writers Church and Conger explain, members of every company cultivate relationships in their own way, "in how much they value collaboration, and in how much face time is required to get work done and make important decisions. In some organizations, the only way to influence others is by spending time with them in

person. In others, emailing, texting, and video conferencing are preferred over in-person meetings."

You will gather some of this information by watching "where and how your colleagues work and make decisions." Another way is by asking co-workers their best practices for building relationships in your organization. Ask whether you need to take time to know someone before asking for help or to request feedback on a project. Or is it okay there for you to "gather a list of 'go-to' individuals whom you can simply email for assistance when you need them?"[38]

2. **Communications:** How do your coworkers, bosses, and other department or teams communicate with one another around your office? You'll need to observe and learn this right away. Do people have formal, scheduled meetings to make status reports and receive next steps on things? Or is it done more casually, without a lot of paperwork and preparation? Maybe your boss just asks you to come in to the office and fill her in as she needs it, or invites you to join a

conversation that has just come together. Your boss will likely tell you about what he or she expects and prefers, but talk to assistants and other members of your workgroup, department, or team to confirm this and to get the preferences of others in your company.

Regarding other higher-ups in your organization, Church and Conger explain, "Hierarchy often determines when and where it is acceptable to communicate with senior colleagues. For example, in more hierarchical environments, you might have to 'pre-clear' any communications upward in the hierarchy with your boss. In less hierarchical organizations, people may be encouraged to email senior leaders to chat with them."[39] What's your corporate communication mode, do you think?

Also learn what formats your boss and team use to share information—with each other, with their bosses, and across the department. Are there a lot of reports and PowerPoints presenting status and projects and updates, i.e., quite formal? Or "can individuals informally share issues, debate topics, and engage in real-time brainstorming without being judged? Some organizations and departments prefer 50-page presentations with reams of details and analyses, while others prefer to work from a simple emailed agenda with a bulleted list of topics."[40]

Start with how meeting packets are put together, beginning with whether there is a typed agenda, if "issues are debated versus 'checked off,' and how deferential people are to those in positions of power." Are your top bosses or managers more persuaded to act or approve something if it's presented formally or forcefully advocated for? Or do they respond better to a conversational style with various options?

How is everybody else getting things done and making things happen around you? Great to study and emulate!

3. **Decision-making:** Every company and team is going to be different on this topic. Some managers or leaders make their decisions about what's happening next and which things are a go right there in the room, at formal meetings, but others use meetings and

presentations to get ideas out there and then "finalize decisions offline."

In some companies, lots of important decisions get made in the break room, as people pass each other and chat, or when they go out to lunch and take time to talk things over. You'll even want to study if "the decisions made in the meetings get implemented. If you see people agreeing to some set of actions in a meeting, and then notice that other things happen afterward, that suggests there are strong informal decision-making mechanisms at play that you'll need to uncover."[41]

You'll need to get decisions made on your work or passions or direction sooner or later—probably sooner!—so you want to arm yourself with the best strategies for being successful in *your* workplace. Maybe you really need a certain advocate who always has the boss's ear. Or maybe you have to figure out—or already know—if your company culture has a *"bias for action* or a *bias for analysis and consensus."*[42]

Is your organization a place where decisions are made quite quickly? Do you have managers or bosses with shorter attention spaces, who really prefer action over longer contemplation, who tend to just *decide* what should happen? Or is your culture more geared to looking at all the angles before arriving at a determination? Do bosses want options everyone can discuss? Do they like to see models of various paths? Do you need to build consensus by providing documentation and presentations—maybe more than once?

Amazon lists **bias for action** as one of their select few leadership principles, and they share what they mean across their company, so this aspect of their company culture is crystal clear: "Speed matters in business. Many decisions and actions are reversible and do not need extensive study. We value calculated risk taking."[43]

But Amazon is *not* every company! Is yours more like Amazon, however, or more inclined to caution and contemplation? Equally important to ask yourself: "What is your own bias for action, and how does it fit your new culture?"[44]

4. **Individual Versus Group Perspectives.** Is yours a team-oriented organization with collaboration as the chief way it expects work to be done? Or is yours more individualistic in its approach to work, which, Church and Conger say, "will generally support a 'hero mentality' that recognizes the ambitious individual. Rewards are often individually based, and performance management tends to be based on individual ratings, where everyone's unique contribution is justified to their peers."[45]

You can see how these two types of organization—group-focused versus those that flatter the ambitious individual—would appeal to different sorts of workers. The former offers "more of a safety net in that risks and rewards are shared, but it may be harder to stand out as an individual and differentiate yourself. ... If you enjoy individual recognition, you may not get what you need fast enough in terms of career progression."[46]

Is there a lot of "I" talk around meetings and presentations? Or is the emphasis more on group achievements? Those are the two different types of culture, and beyond being aware, for yourself, you'll also need to tailor your speech and orientation to the organization's nature.

Why Is This Important?

Bottom line: when you fit in to your company's culture, you are going to enjoy working there so much more. As Alison Doyle goes on to add, "Employees tend to enjoy work when their needs and values are consistent with those in the workplace. They tend to develop better relationships with coworkers and are even more productive.

"On the other hand, if you work for a company where you *don't* fit in with the company culture, you are likely to take far less pleasure out of your work. For example, if you prefer to work independently but work for a company that emphasizes teamwork (or has shared office spaces), you are likely to be less happy and less efficient."[47]

Is your boss and their management style traditional, for example, with your duties and responsibilities clearly defined? Are you clear about how you can get a raise or promotion? Is it very formal? Or is your culture more casual? Can you just jump on cross-functional teams or take on more responsibility on your own? Where do you fit better?

And if working someplace fun and disruptive is more your style, then you'll definitely want to consider a company's culture before you take a new job or make a move. Your employers are also going to be evaluating if you "fit" with how they manage things, so, if you're in the job market, expect some part of the interview and onboarding process to be around company culture.

How Do I Dig into My Company Culture?

You want to develop a practical, eyes-and-ears attunement to your workplace, department, bosses, and managers. Make it a deliberate process to figure out how it really works.

And remember: your true company culture is not necessarily what is being *said*, either by your manager or HR or the employee handbook. *Sometimes* what's said is what you need to know, but *sometimes* there's a wrinkle to it that, so you'll need to parse or observe it and then act accordingly.

For example, when the boss organizes a bi-monthly phone call with a certain department or project group and *says* the calls are not mandatory *but* she takes roll and registers being upset if you miss it… well, your take-away is, in this culture, you need to make those calls, "mandatory"!

If you work in a hot-climate state like I do, in Florida, and the "official" word is that it's okay to wear shorts to work or go casual on Fridays, observe first whether or not people actually *do* that. If they don't, you don't want to, either. It's not *really* part of this company's actual culture.

The reason why this is important is simple: you will have a better chance at succeeding here, if you know your company culture and swim with it.

Also attune yourself to all the ways your own organization teaches and encourages you to embrace their unique culture and priorities. This will help you at the start of your joining a company, but also in terms of thinking about how to use your company's culture to advance in your career.

Kasey Sixt, VP of CKR Interactive and experienced in decades of HR hiring, outreach, and retention successes, also mentions that, right now, "a lot of companies have career mobility, so they explain how to navigate their own environment and culture. If they're a global company, you just have to navigate to see what boxes you have to check to get to the next level.

"Many of these companies are all about the employee experience and how to retain top talent. So, if you're in a career path and just starting out, you may only think you'll stay at your company two years, but organizations want to show you ways to stay with them and grow there. Find out what to do next to build that career path. Mentors can also help guide you internally (*We'll deep-dive into mentors and sponsors later in the book—Ed.*). But the answer is *not* always that you have to *leave* your company" to acquire the skills, experience, and access steps for your career progression.[48]

Many companies are trying to communicate their culture through a variety of programs, so part of exploring corporate culture is to look into what yours has available. Does your organization have a talent development department? Does your HR department offer specific programs like "My Career: How to Navigate It"? Or is there a combination of formal programs and Affinity or Diversity groups? Many companies now offer University within their company; this combination of online and in-person resources is designed to teach you how to navigate the company and potential career tracks. Plus, it often explains the things you need to do or the skills they're offering to teach you, in order to tick the boxes you'll need for promotion.

Kasey Sixt goes on to remind you that, by drilling down into these aspects of your company—the parts that encourage you to participate and excel in the culture—you are taking ownership of your career. You'll discover the ways your company is interested in accommodating your growth. This is also a way to learn if your workplace has some of the flexibility that is becoming more common now, like working remotely or taking internal or external trainings to qualify for next-level jobs.

In addition to your on-the-job observations, reading, talking to or shadowing people, and watching how things happen day-to-day, there are now resources like Glassdoor.com that publish employee reviews and culture details on lots of companies, including annual rankings; *Business Insider* and *Forbes* also look at best places to work. LinkedIn can tell you a lot through their company profiles and your connections to managers. Plus, their thought leaders often have LinkedIn posts and other content that is very informative.

Sometimes, we think these are resources only for job *seekers,* but you as an employee can bolster your success in the workplace by absorbing all sources of information.

Keep Diving Deep

You'll want to do a lot of this work and research as a new employee, figuring out your corporate culture and how things work. But you will also want to keep attuned to what's going on beyond your team, department, and job arena, in order to excel in your workplace. Take it from Amazon!

Amazon publishes and promotes their company's guiding leadership principles, and one of their top priorities for employees at all levels is **Dive Deep**. What do they mean? "Leaders operate at all levels, stay connected to the details, audit frequently, and are skeptical when metrics and anecdote differ. No task is beneath them."[49]

So, as one young Amazon Web engineer, Corey Salzer, explains, this means you should "not just understand the layer that you're working on, but really what's going on underneath that and around. It's about really understanding the big picture and how things work together and asking a lot of why-type questions."

Follow your own route to cracking corporate culture and staying on top of it.

###

STEP 2

MAKE YOUR BOSS LOOK GOOD

> *"Make the most of yourself by fanning the tiny, inner sparks of possibility into flames of achievement."*
>
> —Golda Meir, fourth Prime Minister of Israel

AS LONG AS WHAT you're doing is legal, making your boss look good is your most important priority. And it's one of the best things you can do for yourself in the workplace: for your future, for your capacity to get things done, for your ability to make things happen.

That's my bottom line for you (then we'll get into the nitty-gritty). Because, when you make your boss look good, you'll be fine in your job. He or she will take care of you (or most of them will!). Let's just say the odds are in your favor, if you master this step and consistently do it well.

But doing this is not negotiable, either way. This is something you *have* to do. Broad strokes, your job, whatever your industry or corporate structure or organization management, is to understand what your boss needs in order to do her or his job well and so he or she looks good — to the board of directors, shareholders, stakeholders, or his or her boss. When he or she looks good, *you'll* do well, too!

Just doing your own job well is not going to cover this Step. It takes awareness of this principle, it takes identifying what your boss needs and how you can help, and then it takes your delivering concrete support, help, responses, recognition — whatever it is. And, most important of all, you cannot be competing with your boss.

First, Get to Know Your Boss

Forbes writer Sarah Lundrum has some great tips on how to "Invest in a Relationship with your Boss." "When you're first hired, you should get to know your company's culture and closely watch your boss as you learn the ropes …

Getting to know your boss begins with knowing how they move through the business day, including their moods, how they prefer to communicate, and their style of leadership.

"**Mood:** Perhaps your boss needs their cup of coffee to start the day. If you see other employees scurry away before the boss drains that cup of coffee, bide your time, too.

"**Communication:** The boss's communication style is also influenced by their mood. Don't wait too late to break important news. In-depth topics may be scheduled for a meeting through a phone call or email to check in and show you respect your boss's time. In return, your time will be respected, too. Some professionals are more emotionally reinforcing than others. Some might appear cold but, in reality, just prefer to use hard data to solidify the endpoint as an analytical style. If you're more focused on interpersonal relationships, that's your strength, but you must also learn and respect your boss's communication style.

"**Leadership:** What kind of leader is the boss? ... Autocratic leaders assume total authority on decision-making without input or challenge from others. Participative leaders value the democratic input of team members, but final decisions remain with the boss."[50]

Research shows that your attention to your boss's style and needs (so you can deliver what they want from you in the way they can best appreciate) inspires them directly to support you—in your career, your ambitions, in getting things done. *Forbes* adds, "When millennial employees feel supported by their boss, their happiness on the job soars— and so does company success."[51] So, you can even make yourself happier at work by helping your boss succeed!

Let me give you an example from my workplace. I manage a strategic team of people and our responsibilities often involve travel, outreach, and events all over the country. At the moment, we are short one person and another has her travel delimited by a health situation. This means for me, as the team leader, *and for my boss*, who is always the top consideration as the head of the USTA, there are events we can't cover in the way we would like to cover them.

Now, I happen to have a team member whom I've been considering for promotion. She does her particular job well, but she hasn't demonstrated a great deal of self-awareness in this particular situation and hasn't jumped in to fill some of the gaps we're experiencing. Even when I ask her to take on a few more events, since we don't have the capacity to cover them otherwise, she has resisted adding to her regular workload.

There are a couple of consequences to this. First, my entire team has to scramble when she either doesn't volunteer to help us out or won't find a way to add temporarily to her basic job scope.

But more important, I am much less likely now, as her manager, to put her forward for a promotion, because she hasn't demonstrated her understanding that she needs to change up her approach to work while things are different in our staffing situation. She has not yet learned how important it is to shift her lens from not just doing her job well to figuring out how she can help her boss (in this case, me), so I look okay and my work shines which, in turn, makes *my* boss look even more okay—where we are well-represented in the field, touch all the stakeholders we're in business to engage, and maximize our professional profile while realizing the USTA mission through these particular programs.

So that's how it works... If you aren't being put forward for promotion, could it have to do with not being in tune with your boss and what makes her or him look great?

Not Sure How? Try These!

There are a lot of great questions you can (and should!) ask your boss, some when you first start out, but others you can ask on a regular basis. One of them absolutely *is:*

"What can I do to make you more successful today (or this week, month, quarter, or year)?"[52]

In your regular efforts to make your boss as successful as possible, his or her direct answers to this question will make for really useful information! Once you know your boss's responses, you will know how to focus your energy and time and priorities (we'll talk about setting work priorities under "Crushing Core Competencies"). Asking this question directly also provides your boss feedback, because it verbalizes your adherence to this Step, this principle, that your work isn't *just* your work. Your boss's looking good is your work, too.

What your boss needs you to do, in order to do well and look great, is going to vary, of course, from person to person, business to business. But here are a few tips from Monster.com to get you started.[53] Can you try out any of these? And then put some new ones on your own list?

1. **Discover What the Boss Needs Before They Know They Need It.** You can assume yours, like most bosses, doesn't generally have as much time to think ahead as they would like. So, are there prompts or pre-planning you can do in order to help them be super-prepared? Can you make folders or lists of what your boss needs to know when they come to work tomorrow, for them to review overnight?

2. **Pump Up Your Manager with Useful Research.** Can you do the deep preparation before your boss meets new clients or customers or goes into a meeting about a new opportunity? Can you offer ideas for their

strategy or conversation by doing the research legwork and writing it up for them, in advance?

3. **Take on the Details so Your Boss Can Focus on the Big Picture.** How much of a project's paperwork and details can you handle? Can you see how your freeing up a boss's time to do strategy, relationship-building, or top-line management will make them look great?

4. **Fill in the Boss's Gaps.** Bosses don't *know* everything! And they can't *be* everywhere. Plus, as management consultant Billie Blair reminds us, "Every boss will have things they ought to do but prefer not to do."[54] So, can you notice what your boss isn't getting to do as fast as they should, like answering all the calls and emails or doing certain administrative paperwork? Can you do that stuff?

5. **Help Your Boss Keep Her/His Promises.** Stay attuned to commitments your boss makes in writing, emails, calls, or meetings. If they don't seem to happen soon thereafter, ask about them or set up a way to track actionable items.

6. **Keep Your Boss on Time.** Everyone looks good when they stay on schedule and are prompt for meetings or calls. How can you help your boss do this? Maybe holding up new phone calls, so they have time to get to the next event. Maybe slipping a note in to them to wrap-up a meeting. Maybe preparing a typed or electronic schedule for their desk or phone with notifications. Find their style then help them out!

7. **Polish Your Boss's Language.** We all need editors, proofreaders, even grammar police here and there. Your boss looks good when their letters, emails, memos, and reports have had a careful eye go over them after they're written. If you were an English major, all the better! You get to use your skills, and your boss will always appreciate the save.

8. **Buff Your Boss's Presentations.** Mastering PowerPoint and other presentation skills will support your boss's message and expand their capacity to communicate and succeed. Lend your hand at the visuals, organization, proofreading, dynamic video—

anything you can contribute that amplifies your boss's pitch. Everyone on the team wins!

9. **Anticipate Issues.** Be your boss's eyes and ears. Notice what's happening and perhaps look out to the horizon, while they're focused on their core work. And where you can make suggestions to head off a problem, all the better!

10. **Represent the Boss's View of Corporate Culture.** You are an extension of your boss—with colleagues; in your department and others; out in the field—and a reflection of them, so it behooves you to project a positive image. Make sure anything that represents the team—whether it's an e-mail or a voice mail coming from you—also reflects you and the boss in a professional, polished way.[55] Align your vision with her or his priorities for your organization's culture, and implement it like you were the boss![56] Even if your boss would do things a different way, you are an extension of her or him, in the workplace and in public, so you want to take care of whomever they would take care of just as well as they would.

So, what's on your list of to-dos for your boss? What happens when you're more aware of making the boss shine?

The Muse writer Jessica Kleiman reminded me of that funny scene in *The Devil Wears Prada* where top fashion editor Miranda Priestley (played by Meryl Streep) is walking through a fancy party with her brilliant assistant Andrea (Anne Hathaway) by her side, as Andrea whispers the name and juicy facts about each guest just before Miranda swoops up to them like she knows and remembers them all so perfectly.[57]

You get a chance to make your boss's life easier, too, in your own business and your own way. Kleiman has another five steps to help you accomplish this important Step #2:

1. "Go Beyond Your Job Description." Be prepared to show you're up for the challenge by volunteering to take on more than you're expected to do. What tasks does your boss have to do that you can take on? Add this to the questions you ask her or him. Maybe they won't be the most challenging or interesting things you do all day, but your boss will look better both by

those things getting done *and* by having more time and energy to do other work that help make his or her boss look great.

2. "Pay Attention to Detail." With so much information coming in and out of our phones, computers, and desks and with so many answers needed so quickly, sometimes even our bosses don't think everything through before replying to an email or text. Where can you provide quality-control, helping your boss and her team check for errors on proposals, memos, presentations, and correspondence? And where can you help your boss by slowing down, yourself? Always double check or reread an email or reply before you hit "send." Use other people on your team to proofread things you're writing for the boss.

3. "Let the Boss Know About Mistakes Before His or Her Boss Finds Out." If your supervisor gets called out on something she didn't know about ahead of time, it makes her seem like she's not on top of what's going on. And when she looks bad, trust me, you do, too. So,

the next time you screw up, 'fess up fast, and offer to fix it.

4. "Stay Up on the Latest Trends." It's hard for busy bosses to stay up on what's happening in your industry and related areas, like new technologies, marketing techniques, or real-time data. But you can stay plugged in and then share, or send your boss a link on some great article or interview with an industry thought leader he might have missed, especially if it could help your team or project. Note things your boss might not be aware of and would help your department be more cutting-edge or ahead of the curve. Kasey Sixt of CKR encourages you to "even offer to train her or him on a new social media platform like Periscope. He'll look like he's on top of his game, and he'll recognize you as the reason for that."[58]

5. "Bring Solutions instead of Problems." Everyone—including the boss—has to do more with less these days. When part of your job is managing people, you can end up spending a lot of your time just putting out

fires, resolving conflicts, and trying to deliver the core products or services. Save your boss time and energy by coming up with potential solutions to whatever challenge you're facing. Try saying to him, "I have a problem. Here's how I would propose handling it. What do you think?" This can really help out your boss—and makes a new part of you shine, at the same time!"[59]

###

STEP 3

WHO ARE THE COMPANY "PLAYERS"?

"The fastest way to change yourself is to hang out with people who are already the way you want to be."

—Reid Hoffman, LinkedIn co-founder

IN ANY COMPANY we work at, there are top players: key individuals who either lead the most people, head up the best-funded initiatives, have the boss's or the board of directors' ear, and/or really get stuff done!

The top boss is one of these people, of course, but there are always others. Organizations are big places; there are generally numerous people who stand out in any enterprise, accomplishing some key aspects of the mission or business plan. Wherever you are in your own company, you have many, many reasons to figure out who the players are.

Who's Tied to What Matters?

Remember when you did some research and investigated what matters to your organization? That information is unique to where you work. Keeping it in mind will open many doors for you.

Refer back to those primary initiatives, areas, and priorities. Now, who are the people you see as key to the success of your organization, particularly around delivering on those things that matter? They could be the project directors. They could be the top sellers of your products or raise the most money for what programs or services your company wants to provide. They could be the boss's right-hand person. Whoever they are, *you* need to identify them, first of all. Know who they are.

Second, be mindful: you don't want to cross them. You don't want to get on their bad side, you don't want to ignore a request or a task from them, and you likely don't want to gossip about or criticize them, even when they're not around. (It *always* gets back to them…)

And third, if you can begin to find ways to form some work-related relationships with them, that will bode well for your being able to make things happen for you and your boss. After analyzing the outcomes of your organization's budget and priorities and then identifying who is connected to them, can you try to find ways to help those key people? Are there ways to get your things done by bringing them somehow into the orbit of a key or influential player or project?

If you can help them achieve something they want to achieve, the value of your stock goes up. And they're going to want you around them. They'll want you to be in their circle. Everybody is looking out for themselves, but they'll know you are looking out for them, as well. It is always good to help one of your company's key people achieve what they're trying to achieve. And that's a way to achieve what you want to achieve, too.

For an example, with our organization, the USTA, (like many others), revenue is a huge priority. So, naturally, the person who brings in revenue through our largest and most prominent program, the U.S. Open, is one of the people who matters most here. Period. Also, the woman who runs all of professional tennis serves a very important function. Our U.S. Open program is under her jurisdiction. She is a key figure. Also, I mentioned earlier our new youth tennis initiative, Net Generation. Now, the man who runs this program may not have the seniority of many other folks at the USTA—he's been here about two years—but because the *program* is a big deal for us, *he's* a big deal here. If there happens to be an extra $100 in the budget, maybe I can commandeer a piece of it for my division, but chances are he'll get most if not all of it.

In order to make things happen for me and my department at the USTA, I need to know these basic facts: *what* matters to my organization and *who* is tied to those initiatives. That will also lead me to know in any instance or meeting or budget discussion, if there is going to be a challenge for resources or direction, these three people will have more power and influence than I will by dint of what they do vis á vis the USTA's mission and priorities.

You will also notice, in companies and associations, things can ebb and flow, go in and out of favor or emphasis or urgency. By the same token, certain people in an organization can be hot sometimes—on a selling streak or high in influence with the top management—and then, at other times, not so much. These are thing you need to observe, make note of, and really understand! Keep your eyes and ears attuned to what's what. It will really make a difference for your success in the workplace.

Who's Your Keymaster?

You know how Chipotle and Peet's coffee and Jamba Juice have secret menus? (Fruity Pebbles or Dirty Chai, anybody?) Well, your office or organization has its own secrets, too—their ways of doing things (like you're figuring out by studying your corporate culture) and who matters. But another person who matters is someone who may not be in top management or leadership, but they are important for you to connect with because they are the person or people who "know(s) the code" in the company. There is usually one in every organization and sometimes more than one.

These are the individuals, according to Jennifer Winter in *Skirts & Suits,* who "always seem to have dibs on all the great projects, front-row seats in the important meetings, and opportunities to advance into positions that no one else even knew existed."[60]

How can you find out the "unwritten rules of your office"? Winter calls the person "who's always the first to know the biggest news and always has the ear of the boss ... The one who's typically involved in a little bit of everything—and always the big stuff," the **Keymaster**, the person who really knows the inner workings of your organization.

It makes sense you should find this person and get to know them, along with your boss and the top movers and shakers. You may even have seniority to him or her and decide not to make an effort to build a relationship with them... Not smart! There is a big downside to being out of the loop that your company's Keymaster controls. And even your boss is likely to know the upside to staying in their good graces!

So, can you figure out who is "the heart and soul of your office"? Can you find a way to get to know them, maybe help them out? As Winter describes, "Do this right, and in time, you'll start to see a few of your office secrets revealed."

You can learn seemingly minor things that will make your office hum (and smell) better, like the protocols for the break room microwave and refrigerator. But also, by paying close attention to the keymaster in various situations, you can discern "what time to show up for a team meeting, what to order (or not) when out to lunch with clients," and many more quirks and success strategies for your company.[61]

When You're Not with the Movers & Shakers

Not everyone in an organization has a boss or department that is the current favorite of the movers and shakers… That is just fine. You can still make lots of things happen—for your mission, for your career, and in your workplace.

I know because, as a head of Diversity & Inclusion, I am fully aware my department is not the main money-maker or even the capstone project of an organization like the USTA. However, by paying close attention to *what* and *who* matters, along with the remaining Steps for success in this book, I am able to advance my projects, do work that really excites and matters to me, and find excellent ways to help each of those top players through D&I. (We'll talk about D&I and how *you*, too, can leverage it as one of your Core Competencies, in the next chapter.)

What this has meant, being part of a department that is not the go-to place, per se, for funding and resources or PR and praise, is that our team just works harder to make what matters to us seem sexy *and* to show everyone in the organization how it can advance their success. You can always collaborate with the people who matter, once you figure them out, and do your own great things—important work. You'll just be able to do more, faster, better, and get more satisfaction and notice if you stay aware of who matters and how you can work with them.

STEP 4

CRUSH YOUR CORE COMPETENCIES

"Some people dream of success, while other people get up every morning and make it happen."

—Wayne Huizenga, owner, the Miami Dolphins

THIS IS GOING TO BE either the most obvious Step for you or the most helpful. Either way, I'm sure you are already an expert at some of these skills and competencies I'm going to enumerate below. But you may not have been taught others, or you can focus on brushing up on them, so you are the total package to make things happen.

Bottom line: in your first jobs, in order to do your work well, to be promoted, to really be successful in an organization, you need to develop all the proper competencies. My list for you is long! But it is infinitely doable and directly connected to producing solid results as well as forging a great career in the work and field you love.

So, here are the Top 15 Things You Need to Do Well!

1. Develop Knowledge of Self

You always need to be honest with yourself about who you are, what you're good at, and what you're not so great at. Yes, we're all always working on ourselves and remaining positive, but you will be able to go far when you really know these specifics unique to you and then take things from there.

This can be a challenging competency, but it can actually work well for you. For example, when I was a kid playing competitive tennis, I knew through practice and coaching what I was really good at. But I *also* knew what I was not as strong at doing. Trust me, if I tried doing the not-so-good shots or techniques or approaches during a match, things did *not* work out for me! Know your strengths. Be aware of who you are.

If you are a great presenter like Steve Jobs and can always move a room, that's great. But, of course, not everyone can do that. If you can't, you need to know this before you jump in and *try*! (Below, we talk about the kinds of professional development you can do, like learning to make presentations and think creatively, so you develop and practice these skills. But first, know what you know and do well.)

Always know which skills are your strongest and which you either need to practice and develop or work around.

2. Learn to Manage Up

This will help you get answers, results, and action steps from your boss or bosses—the people above you and/or to whom you report—so you can move your own agenda forward and deliver what your boss needs. Yes, you would think your boss would make it easy to deliver what she needs! But managers are busy people with many pulls on their time and attention. When you are managing up well, you can get in and out with the information you need rather than get bottlenecked or stymied by procedure or personality.

On my team, I have an employee who is particularly good at managing up—in other words, in handling *me*. If I'm not responding to a question/memo/something she needs done or if I'm not giving her what she needs on a timely basis so she can keep doing her own job well, she knows how to get me to take action, provide answers, and keep her particular work moving forward. For her success, this is a vital skill.

How does she do it? Well, sometimes she can get me to take action first by reminding me a decision is needed *and also* by giving me two to three recommendations or options. As a manager, it is much easier to choose what to do efficiently from a vetted list rather than have to generate the options, myself. In addition, she always includes her own recommendation, detailing how it would work, while also explaining how the other choices would work, as well. In this way, she ensures I am thinking about everything pertinent in order to help keep the project or decision moving forward.

(In this instance, it was something I needed to do regarding her professional development plan (PDP); she needed to ensure it got done for herself, personally, but seeing it through was also good for our department. This strategy, however, applies whenever you need a boss's answer on anything, maybe from another department or an outside stakeholder; or when he needs to set a meeting or set time to review a presentation, etc. In any instance, like my employee, you just want to be sure your boss has everything they need to ensure the job gets done!)

Other ways of managing up include developing the agenda for a meeting of your boss and her project team. You can help drive the meeting so you are incorporating your boss's suggestions about how to proceed, but be sure you have already prepared counter-suggestions with *rationale*, so you help manage your boss to a choice or decision you believe in. You can suggest your boss might want to think about anything, including his own suggestion, a certain way and always include why you think so. This is a strategy that really works!

Part of mastering this general competency is something very specific to you and your bosses. You want to get to know how the other person or people tick, and what rhythms and strategies work best with *them*. Then you also want to provide options in any situation where you need their decision. You can always try to steer your manager toward what you recommend or believe to be the best option, but start managing your boss by giving them possibilities and choices, in order to get to yes. You'll be much more successful than saying, "We just have to do it this way."

3. Manage Your Time

To be successful in your work, you must be able to prioritize. This includes planning your day and your week and your month. Likely you have experience with this, through school and other jobs. Your learned strategies for project planning will become very, very handy, so polish them up or make them even better.

It is very easy to come into your place of work in the morning and be thrown off course, if you don't have a plan for what you're trying to get done, what needs to get done, and what you're going to do next and next. You'll become more skilled at making adjustments, at rescheduling (but not procrastinating!), and at figuring out how much time you need to take care of top priorities plus which need a bit more TLC and attention.

But make it your business to use calendars, agendas, lists, and even time-sheets, to chart out how you will get your work and project and tasks accomplished for your company. And never hesitate to ask. If your boss comes in with a big emergency project, small or long-term, ask how to prioritize it vis á vis the other things on your agenda for the day, week, and month. Those are always great conversations to have: you look responsive, adaptive, and on the learning curve; and you'll get clear input into what to do first, second, and last, without having to guess!

Eventually, you'll just know. You'll even be setting agendas and priorities for a team you manage yourself soon. But up front, get this down. Because as we discuss in one of the last Steps, you need to do all your work, do it well, and deliver what's needed. This skill is your way to get good at doing that.

4. Learn to Communicate Effectively

No doubt you already understand that communication is not just talking; in fact, that's the least of it! Equally important is listening, *really* listening. The fact is, if you listen, people will tell you everything you need to know — especially their pain points, and what they're trying to get done. But you will not hear them if *you're* talking too much.

The *Wall Street Journal* published an influential article a few years ago called, "How Well Are You Listening?" about "active listening." You can still hunt it down online, and it's worth reading, because it has some great details and an infographic that teaches a lot of tips you can adopt and practice.

WSJ points out that "experts say we're naturally just not good at listening for a whole range of reasons"! These include a tendency to interrupt, because a lot of our conversation is swapping stories; our discomfort with emotion, which leads to our resistance to tuning in to a speaker's feelings; and we all love to talk about ourselves, so we urge speakers to hurry through what they have to say so we can have our turn. And sometimes we just have so much experience with self-absorbed speakers, leading to what they call "listener burnout," that we don't let ourselves get put upon by then, but consequently develop defense mechanisms regarding hearing people out.[62]

Check out the story's suggestions for how to really engage in a conversation, from practicing what experts call "immediacy behaviors" like putting away distracting cell phones, leaning in, making eye contact, encouraging your speaker, and paraphrasing so they know you've heard them.

For your work, and in many of the Steps coming up, you'll find this skill helps you learn so much about people and situations. All this comes in very handy.

5. Be Able to Present

Presenting well is an essential skill, and while some students develop presentation experience in college, everyone can keep refining this until they are super-competent and confident about standing up in front of a group, small or large, and presenting a paper, selling a project, providing a clear status update, or arguing effectively for an approach or strategy.

In most communities, there is a Toastmasters International chapter or club, the non-profit educational organization that teaches public speaking and leadership skills through their worldwide network. In these groups, "members improve their speaking and leadership skills by attending one of the 16,600 clubs in 143 countries that make up their global network of meeting locations. ... By regularly giving speeches, gaining feedback, leading teams, and guiding others to achieve their goals in a supportive atmosphere, leaders emerge from the Toastmasters program."[63]

I encourage you to investigate this, whether you have a lot of presentations under your belt so far or not. In addition, there are most likely groups at work that can offer you really good, practical experience at developing this core competency.

For example, most of you will have access to networking and employee resource groups within your organization. Get involved! And not just for the meet-and-greets or social activities. Join up and try to volunteer or be elected to a leadership role, because in doing so, you will have opportunities to present your ideas, both within and outside of those group meetings. Each one of these is invaluable practice for your presentation skills.

6. Be Able to Write Well

Writing is something we study and develop in school but that can always get better with practice. Keep practicing! By yourself, brush up on the basic principles of writing, grammar, and spelling. Continue to read good writing, to practice writing drafts of proposals and presentations and papers, and then find a partner or group to meet with and share writing back and forth, to see if you are communicating your points well, developing a clear but lively style, and avoiding obvious errors of punctuation and word choice.

As Dan Shewan suggests on the *Word Stream* blog, consider dissecting writing you find powerful or exceptional. Even try mimicking writers and styles that really work for you. And *outline*. Even short projects and letters can benefit from thinking through, in advance, how you want to open, express your main thoughts and in what order, summarize, and close out.[64]

7. Learn How to Sell

It's really important to be able to sell your ideas. And yourself. And your company's mission. Be sure you are aware of this, that you know your strengths and weaknesses in selling, and then make it a priority to develop this competency. You need this skill—and not just in retail! You'll need a developed power of persuasion for colleagues to "buy" your approach to things or, say, as in my professional capacity, to convince other departments and stakeholders to adopt the Diversity & Inclusion that means so much to me. I know how to sell it, because I know how to make it something that benefits them.

In my experience, the easiest way to sell is to ask questions and listen to what people are telling you. If you listen to what people are telling you (especially through "active listening," as described above), people will tell you what their pain points are and exactly what they're looking for. They'll tell you precisely what you need to build, what service you need to offer, and how to approach them in order to make a sale to them or their company.

I have two additional tricks, in addition to active listening, that get people to tell me how I can sell something to them. If I don't know exactly, after listening to a potential customer or client, how to approach "selling" them my program or product, I'll ask one or both of these things: First, "Tell me more"; and, "Give me an example."

I have found, even when I'm having a respectful disagreement with someone or just not clear about what someone is criticizing or where they're having a problem with me, I'll say, "Okay, give me two examples." When someone can respond to that, I guarantee you'll know exactly what they're talking about. And then you have something to work with that just can't be parsed when all you've heard is a generality.

Sales is really about dealing with others' problems and finding ways your product, service, or approach can make their lives easier. You want to begin by listening to what your customers or colleagues describe as their unique pain points. Then you want to try and solve that challenge. This is what results in a sale. You will rarely succeed when trying to sell something if you don't even know whether the other party wants or needs it!

You're going to be tasked with selling many things in your workplace. That is very much the nature of work. Maybe it's your program's priorities. Maybe it's your need for an assistant or a bigger budget. Personally, when I have to sell things to my own boss, including a new staff hire, I always start with the strategies we discussed under Managing Up.

I'll use strategies to convince him I need the latitude to hire, say, a manager to replace a departing coordinator, but always in terms of making things look and work better for him and *his* company. I sell him by offering two or three ways to approach this situation but then I'll also add, since he's hired me to do my best, I support a particular approach and then attest to what we need now, in terms of staffing, and why, in order to ensure *he's* doing well in this area. When selling something to my boss, whenever I can still *make it about him,* I generally succeed.

My boss knows as well as I, if I'm doing a great job, he's doing a great job. When you can build a way to make your boss—or anyone!—look good through what and how you're selling, you amplify your chances for getting what you want.

8. Priority Setting

Develop a practice for setting priorities for your work. First, zero in on critical priorities. These go at the top of your list, of course. Now figure out how to break those down and schedule them out, with targets and deadlines over time.

First, consider what should be your priorities for the year—a full 365 days. Then, list your monthly, weekly, and daily priorities.

The key to setting priorities and making them happen is always to keep the end in mind: identify what *has* to get done and then figure out what it is you have to do, in order to accomplish that goal or get where you need to get.

Take a few moments before each day's work to identify what it is that you are going to do today. Also, not anything that may be getting in the way of attaining any of your benchmarks or time goals.

Now, of course, your boss is going to be a heavy influence on your priorities. She may even set most of them, herself. Those are the things you must do first! But do check, maybe at the end of each week and month, that your boss's priorities and projects are basically in line with what you are trying to get done, yourself, as an individual. If you find too often that his or her priorities are not working for you or in conflict with what you believe you should be doing, you may need to ask yourself whether you are in the right job.

These check-ins are part of nailing your skills at setting priorities. And conflicts will arise. Take an example from my "world." Let's say your personal objective is to be a top-ranked tennis player, but your coach regularly assigns you to all doubles games. Here you would see that your priorities are not aligned with your coach's, and the two of you are not a professional fit. So always go back to that first chapter: Know what you ultimately want. Then keep your priorities in mind!

9. Be Results Oriented

The idea behind doing proper planning is getting results. You must continue to develop your mastery of setting goals and measuring progress against those goals—weekly, monthly, and annually for as far out as ten years. When you are clear about the results you want and need, it will become very clear what you're not attaining, which gives you an opportunity to re-evaluate. Maybe you need to pivot, like the tennis player in my example above. Maybe you need to retool your skills or even your basic goals.

Being results-oriented speaks to the language of business, so develop this habit sooner rather than later. You will be seen as someone who is focused, with their eye on the ball, and able to clearly measure success, in the end. I can tell you this, as a boss: if you tell me what success will look like and how we can measure or monitor success out of funds in my budget, that becomes an excellent ask for funding and resources on something you want to do!

Learn how to measure your work—this is the metric component of being results-oriented. Learn how to monitor your process, your progress, and your results on any project, program, or endeavor. Practice setting clear, measurable, *SMART* goals, i.e., ones that are Specific, Measurable, Attainable, Realistic, and Time-sensitive.

Amazon puts "**Deliver Results**" as one of its top, published leadership principles. They define it for their entire team this way: "Leaders focus on the key inputs for their business and deliver them with the right quality and in a timely fashion. Despite setbacks, they rise to the occasion and never settle."[65]

One current employee, Corey Salzer, who landed a great Web Services job at Amazon right out of college, leveraged the company's 14 leadership principles in order to impress recruiters, starting with how to apply "Deliver Results." She suggests one way to show how you are personally committed to delivering results, either in an interview or even job review with your boss or team leader, is to try using this phrase:

"I was able to have a lot of responsibility and decision-making ability for X project, and by doing Y tasks, I delivered results in Z number of launches." In the same way, also explain any setbacks your project faced and/or how those were turned around.[66]

10. Organizational Agility

This skill is about how to get things done within your organization, through both formal and informal channels. In our early chapters, we looked at figuring out what matters to your company, what they publish, and how they present their priorities and mission, plus what they *don't* tell you, as well as who matters and really gets things done. Mastering this information and then leveraging it to become stronger in your workplace is what this competency is all about.

You will have occasion to work through both formal and informal channels, so you need to know how to do both.

Armed with a solid understanding of your organization, you will have the insight as to which of these two approaches you should choose, in order to solve any given problem or to advance a certain initiative/agenda. In any given work situation, you need the ability to develop the best strategy for efficiency and success by applying the available and appropriate levers.

This starts with knowing how to get your boss to move on something. Is this an instance where you present the information right up front, including your recommendation and a few options? Or would it be better to wait for him to come around to considering this issue, himself, and be more indirect?

11. Customer Focus

This is a competency, a strategy, a work philosophy that truly applies to everything we do in business. For anything you and your organization do, sell, or service, you must constantly ask what they—your customer, your stakeholders, your partners—want and need, including how they would like it given or supplied to them.

Whether your business is product-based or service-oriented, a customer focus means that everyone, from owners and top management to your team and department, is committed to ensuring that all aspects of the company put its customers' satisfaction first. Often this also involves an organization having a dedicated customer-relations department and service program, but the responsibility is spread to *everyone* in effective, successful companies.

The mindset of leaders in any company evolves from a sales philosophy. No matter the industry, they want their team to help their customers achieve whatever the organization's goals and objectives are. Once you identify who your personal customers are, you are constantly asking:

- ➢ What is in it for them?
- ➢ How can you help them?

And if you can't deliver what they need, having a customer focus also means you let them know that, and why! Effective communication with your customers on all topics is a key part of customer focus.

Amazon developed fourteen leadership principles, which they posted to their entire team,[67] and the very first principle is "customer obsession." They explain it this way: "Leaders start with the customer and work backwards. They work vigorously to earn and keep customer trust. Although leaders pay attention to competitors, they obsess over customers."

Corey Salzer, a 23-year-old solutions architect at Amazon Web Services, suggested mentioning these leadership principles in an applicant's résumé, cover letter, and interview, as a major way to impress recruiters, and then to connect Amazon's principles back to a project or team you were involved with, even in school or at an internship. It was how she landed her job at the company right out of college.

"Customer obsession is the really big one. We focus on Amazon's customers," Salzer said, "and always work backwards from what they need and what they're doing." During her own Amazon interview right out of college, before she landed her job, Salzer emphasized how she and her team focused on the needs of her users and customers while designing a product.[68]

As you develop this competency personally, look for the indicators and thought leaders in your organization who define customer focus as it pertains to your business and field. Notice how you can learn to anticipate and then meet whatever your unique customers need and then begin to support your organization in its goals to exceed these needs. Doing so will also require effective communication, particularly your active listening skills.

12. Interpersonal Savvy

A core competency for any employee who hopes to do well and rise in an organization is to constantly develop and refine your awareness of the people around you, whether above or below you, peers or customers, and then to consciously approach situations with a smart strategy for accomplishing what you want from people.

Your interpersonal skills are the tools you use to interact and communicate with people in your workplace. You want to consider and refine your abilities in these seven areas, some of which we have touched on as other competencies:

- ✓ Verbal communication—your ability to communicate through words with the correct tone and manner.
- ✓ Non-verbal communication, which includes facial expressions, body language, and hand gestures; these can be read or interpreted as positive or distinctly negative, even when words are saying the opposite.
- ✓ Listening skills—as mentioned around active listening, you need to be able to hear things attentively and then process what you hear.
- ✓ Negotiation—you to need to be able to talk things out and come to an agreement on next steps or policy. This means developing a professional approach to listening, discussing, and then coming up with solutions that work for all parties in a situation.
- ✓ Problem-solving—the ability to find a solution to a problem after considerable thought; pulling

together all the variables that make up both a challenge and the way ahead, to fix, advance, or change it up.

- ✓ Decision-making—sometimes we make decisions quickly; other times, it's best *not* to decide! But generally, in order to make a choice or come to a conclusion, you'll apply a variety of interpersonal skills, starting with fact-finding, and then use logical thinking, creativity, and your analytical ability. Coming to the best decision also include sensitivity to others in the process.[69]
- ✓ Assertiveness—you've heard it before: you have to speak up, feel confident as you present your case, and not be too easily swayed, when you've done your homework or need to defend your rights.[70]

These interpersonal skills (soft skills), unlike some of your more technical or hard skills, are something you use every day in the workplace, so it's a very good idea to work on analyzing and developing your own strengths and areas to practice. These also lead to developing other important life skills, so your refinement will pay off.[71]

Then, in each of your workplace exchanges, make it your responsibility to keep in mind, as you go into the transaction, conversation, or conflict:

> What are the various ways to approach this situation?

> How can I exercise tact in my approach to this individual?

> How can I employ diplomacy?

> How can I anticipate where problems may arise or where the landmines lie?

In most every workplace, at some point, you are going to encounter an individual who is difficult to get along with. And you're still going to have to deal with them, if not daily then likely around something you need to do or say or negotiate, in order to get your job done.

Given this obstacle or difficult person, your approach *could* be:

❖ To throw your hands up

❖ To figure out how to diffuse the situation, and how to do so without raising your voice…

❖ Or just to avoid arguments over anything with them, ever.

Bottom line, interpersonally speaking, you want to avoid personality conflicts at work. Even when you're clearly right, more competent, better, whatever—always keep in mind, when dealing with difficult people, that you are trying to win the war. You need to get your job done and make things happen. You may be able to win a battle with this person, but that win will invariably jam you up in the long run.

And you know what? Even if your boss doesn't get along with someone, that doesn't mean *you* don't have to dislike or be in conflict with them.

This competency of interpersonal savvy also involves being self-aware, as we discussed up under being an adult at work, as you develop your brand. Think long-term. In organizations everywhere, people you don't like and people who don't like you *must* be able to work together. What can you do to make that happen?

Start by developing your ability to size people up. This is something you should recognize you're doing actively. At the core of your analysis is identifying how you can help each person you work with and assessing how you'll *get along*, not be in conflict.

It will always be the case that the more you know about the people you are working with, the better. This includes how to connect with them and what may or may not work, when you approach them with an ask or an offer. Some organizations and departments use formal Business Personality Assessments, like Myers-Briggs or DISC; the results of these written survey-type personality and style analyses tend to show not just where you place on their charts in terms of style and temperament, but also where others in your group lie, and then how those different types best interact one with the other.

There's nothing wrong at all with these, so take advantage of them, if you're offered. They tend to identify how you like to be communicated to as contrasted with how others do, as well as your problem-solving styles and the processes you lean toward, in arriving at a decision. The idea is to figure out how to approach bosses, colleagues, and clients in the way that works best for *them*, as opposed to our natural tendency; before we size people up, we're going to tend to us only the communication strategy that happens to work best for you, but you can become adept at other approaches, with awareness and practice.

Learn a variety of approaches in developing your interpersonal competency. Practicing this skill can be very powerful in getting done what you hope to accomplish. It's one of the things you just have to have down, in order to excel.

13. Diversity and Inclusion

This is not just my business. This is something, in the 21st century, that is good for your business, for your boss's business, for *everyone's* business. And when you develop a D&I strategy for yourself and others, so that you really understand what it means and how to nurture it, as a core competency, you put yourself in a highly competitive place with advantages for both you and whatever you seek to do.

So, first, bottom line, we live in a multi-cultural, multi-ethnic society, and our economy is being driven by diverse customers, diverse talent, and a diversifying workforce. The changing demographics in the United States mean diversity is a reality we must, and should, deal with. Having an appreciation of others cultures and all types of folks, trying to recognize how this figures in your professional and personal life, is important for your personal development. Having the mindset of not just understanding but leveraging diversity for positive business impact is a home run.

Understanding diversity means acknowledging and leveraging similarities and differences in your clients, colleagues, and service communities. It is a key lever for companies to increase creativity and innovation within their organization and to attain the recruitment and retention of top talent. Diversity is what gives you, your boss, and your entire enterprise access to a changed marketplace.

I teach (and practice) how to keep diversity in mind in the way you select and lead teams, which will be important as you become more of a manager or project participant at work. As you become very savvy about diversity, you will see (and can show your company) how it vastly improves your ability to leverage your resources in order to outperform your competitors.

Diversity *also* has a social component; it involves *inclusion* and *respect*. So, become attuned to how you and your organization value and include any and all individuals. This means *including* the points of view and practices of people with different experiences or backgrounds throughout your workplace. As you and your team become more receptive to different ideas, you come up with more creative solutions, you reach a wider service or customer network, *and* you will know you're doing the right thing![72]

As you develop this essential competency and start to see what can be accomplish through a truly diverse workforce, you will discover its benefits are more than just the talent you recruit or work with. This is an amazing business decision for organizations to implement, especially in how it enables them to reach new markets.[73]

So, make it *your* business to develop your awareness and to activate this competency of D&I in your own work.

Now, I know we all have biases around race, culture, ethnicity, and other social or political demarcations. These are sometimes conscious but largely unconscious. Your responsibility is to identify your own biases. You want to know what they are and then figure out how to deal with or accommodate them, in order to do the best for yourself and your company.

I have them, too! For example, I like to hire people from our various USTA sections. Also, I like to hire women over men. (I grew up with two older sisters who had a strong influence over me, so that could be a *reason* for my bias, but I definitely find women I work with more productive, loyal, and responsible for the best work product.) I actually was not aware of either of these tendencies, to be frank. But then someone brought them to my attention and the numbers don't lie: I've done this in my hiring practices for quite some time.

As may be the case for you, these biases were easier for others to see than for me. I had to have it pointed out to me. In fact, the guy who told me sounded surprised when he said, "You didn't know that?"

I did not know that. Everybody else did, though…! So you, too, may need help seeing your blind spots or biases. Ask around. We're going to talk a lot about sponsors and advisors in later Steps, but let's just say here that while what they tell you about your biases may not be gospel, if four or five different people identify the same thing or things about something you do, the chances are these are something to pay attention to!

14. Creative Problem Solving

If you were not trained in this skill, as most science students throughout college, you may not have developed this competency before starting some of your early jobs. But it is valuable and essential in any workplace, particularly in order to make the most appreciated contributions to your boss and field.

Just about everything we have now is the result of someone or some team solving a problem that may or may not have seemed like a problem. They looked at the world creatively and wondered, "Can we do this a different way?"

Creative problem solving starts by framing up your problem and then trying to look beyond the obvious approach, not stopping at the first answers you get. I encourage you, for any real challenge or in the development of a new approach, to keep going. Keep interrogating the situation, asking "why" and "what if" and "why not" of your various alternatives. This process will certainly add to your practicing and then developing competency in this area.

Honest brainstorming with colleagues and bosses is fine as part of problem-solving, including wild speculation or interrogation of an approach, but *only if it works with your company/business unit culture*. Some bosses or supervisors will say, "No idea is a bad idea." First, however, be sure to find out: do they really mean that? Some organizations do *not* really mean it. As we discussed earlier, in figuring out how *your* company works, you need to know the truth about this approach to problem-solving, before you participate in active brainstorming. Of course, in some cases, they really do mean it. It can lead to some very creative—and disruptive—solutions!

As you tackle a problem, try your best to see the hidden crumbs… Identify what potential challenges could arise out of various approaches to how you and your team are to attain something. Then, try to come up with unconventional ways to solve the problem.

In *Business Insider's* podcast about how John Sculley was selected as Apple CEO by Steve Jobs, Sculley talks about his relationship with the inspirational boss and how he was masterful with words, always looking for creative ways to solve problems.[74] Consider the challenge Jobs addressed when he started with the original Sony CD Walkman, which was its own little revolution for taking music with you by putting a disc inside the device. But Jobs found an entirely unconventional way to "take your music with you." As we know, with even his earliest iPods, Apple put **1000** songs in your pocket. Jobs started by looking at this problem sideways and in a very different, creative way. In the end, of course, this led him to develop a product that was much more successful than the competitors' first foray or solution.

As a digital native in the millennial generation, this is a competency you will become especially good at. The

Deloitte 2018 Millennial Survey of 10,455 educated, full-time millennial employees like you across thirty-six countries, reports, "having grown up with computers in their homes and smartphones in their hands, students and young professionals are well aware that the Fourth Industrial Revolution is upon us and that the very nature of work is changing rapidly.[75] Industry 4.0 is characterized by the marriage of physical and digital technologies, such as analytics, artificial intelligence, cognitive computing, and internet of things technology."[76]

I encourage you to develop this creative problem-solving skill in order to be of great use to your organization. It's also going to be pivotal for you and your career.

15. Learning Agility

It is very important to be able to pick up new skills, techniques, and technological upgrades. Start with noticing what you don't know that seems a commonplace skill around your office. If you're not adept at PowerPoint or Excel reports, or if you haven't had opportunity to format a business letter, report, or memo to a professional standard, be sure you run the YouTube or Microsoft tutorial and give it some practice.

Of course, some folks learn these things quicker than others. I encourage you to learn as quickly as you can, but if you are fast at adopting or learning—whether naturally or through concerted practice—that can be a real sweet spot for you and your boss.

And be sure to analyze not just when you're successful at learning or adopting something, but also when you fail. Knowing when you need to iterate or change direction is almost as important as what you learn.

Your facility at utilizing technology is going to be expected in most any workplace these days. A lot of you have experience through school or earlier jobs, but tech has a wide variety of applications and is also constantly being upgraded and invented. It's a core competency to brush up and stay on top of professional technologies, both general and specific to your field. And, of course, we all know that best practices, methods, and technologies are constantly changing. Stay open to change—it's one of the few constants in life!

###

These 15 skills are what any manager in any organization, corporation, or association anywhere considers core competencies for a great employee. These are the things you *have* to be really good at. Maybe not great, not 10 out of 10 on every one of them, but at least measure or develop yourself to be at least a 7 or 8!

In my experience, your boss and organization will tend to measure you only by your lowest rating on these fifteen competencies, unless you are some kind of super-superstar in one area. And generally, if you're really bad at one or two of these things, it's going to get in the way of your advancing in your job and getting things done. Bottom line: you have to be pretty good at all of them.

In truth, you can pick and choose which of these you want to focus on, either to advance to a 10 in a couple or to bring up some of your weakest ones. But just remember: you want to work toward comfort, agility, and mastery of all fifteen.

STEP 5

ADOPT A MENTOR (Or 3!)

"The only way to make sense out of change is to plunge into it, move with it, and join the dance."

—Alan Watts

SOME OF YOU work for companies that have official mentorship programs. That is great luck. Sign up and take advantage. But many organizations don't offer mentorship in a formal, organized way. Either way, you really need a mentor, official or unofficial, to continue your progress inside your company and learn how to make things happen for you and your career.

When you are starting out in a new organization, as we've been talking about, you want to learn the ropes—of your department, company, and whole field—both internal and external. Who can help?

A mentor is someone who advises you from the perspective of knowing how your company or association works. They have perspective on how the organization works, including the things you need to be aware of and what you need to do, in order to be successful there and thrive. Mentors are informative. Mentors answer your questions. And mentors can see into what you're doing and how you're doing it, providing constructive feedback and concrete advice about what you might need to change or develop, in order for you to make progress in your job and career.

Sounds important, right? Institutional knowledge really comes from gaining mentors within your company. And getting a mentor or mentors is up to you, one of my top Steps for making things happen.

As I mentioned, there are many companies with formal mentorship programs, and you should investigate these first, or in addition to the suggestions I'll make below. Other organizations have those affinity, women in leadership, and diversity groups and ERGs I've been talking about. In addition to other benefits, these are another great place to investigate as a source of mentors. And don't limit yourself to thinking about having just one. Perhaps one mentor is great for career planning and strategy, while another is an ideal guide to help you navigate your company culture. Another might be a better fit to meet with and discuss your problems or challenges.

Now, as Jimmy Okuszka writes in *The Muse*, going about asking someone to be your mentor can be a little intimidating, perhaps! But he and I both caution you about letting your fears "prevent you from seeking out someone to lean on, ... (who) can help you get a job, negotiate benefits, figure out your career path, or even guide you through a sticky work situation."[77]

Who Are Mentors?

Let's focus on your company and dial back to our chapter on *who* and *what* matters in your particular organization. You can try to set up a quarterly or monthly meeting with those actual major players!

You need to believe this truth: people *will* share their knowledge, experience, and philosophy, particularly older team members with younger employees, and even like doing so. But *you* have to give them the opportunity! You can then see where it goes from there.

One manager, Alex Osten, began doing this in college, speaking to a dean of her business school who was very interested in students' progress. She found, after setting up regular sit-downs every month or so, he "eventually started talking about me and my aspirations and we built a natural relationship over time."

This account manager notes, "Having someone I admired who I could casually ask for career advice and learn soft skills from was super helpful. I never formally asked him to be my mentor…" She goes on to suggest, "Let the relationship progress naturally. Find someone who has a career you admire and ask to take them to coffee. Asking for casual career advice can be a great gateway into mentorship!"[78]

So, you can have mentoring without a formal agreement or request. You can also try this with people outside your department or company, even outside your field, if you have questions and can develop a rapport. Most senior executives are going to have wisdom that can help you work through situations in your job and career, even if theirs is not the same as yours. You are looking for mentors who can be generous with their time and information—even if it's just twenty minutes every few months—and on whom you can count to be honest with you as well as support and encourage you.

You can even have a mentor you don't meet with, per se, but just have "conversations" with via email or social media. Maybe you met them at a prior job in another city or at school or even connected through the alumni office. We can have remote mentors now! And sometimes they're the best ones—you have time to post your updates and questions to them and they can respond at their leisure; you're not tied to a face-to-face.

A mentor is someone who can show you the ropes, first of all. But yes, people we work with get busy, another reason you would think about having three or four mentors—and they can be unofficial just as well as official.

So, you may find that looking for a *few* mentors will give you a more rounded perspective on what you need to know or how to address a challenge. There are going to be many aspects of your job and career, so different mentors will have a variety of expertise, access, and knowledge.

TV editor Daniel Zana, interviewed by *The Muse's* Jimmy Okuszka, recommends, "Get a lay of the land and try to get a sense of who you can ask for what. And remember that by asking questions, you not only will learn new things, but you're showing engagement and interest in the job you're doing."[79]

It is also good to think in terms of more than one because you may find that, say, two or three of them are clearly aligned around what your mission is and what you're trying to accomplish. But, over time, you notice another one of them isn't in line so much. That's fine. Although undoubtedly that mentor likes you and means well in how they advise you, maybe that's not the one you listen to quite so ardently…

###

Another great thing about internal mentors or someone who mentors you from a volunteer group or ERG is, as they get to know you, they will become your sponsors and future job references, over time. The key here is, if they know you, they will be able to sponsor and/or recommend you without your knowledge. You *want* that.

Let's look at developing sponsors in the next Step.

STEP 6

CULTIVATE A SPONSOR

"Respect is earned, Honesty is appreciated. Trust is gained. Loyalty is returned."

—Oscar Auliq-Ice

IN SOME WAYS, a sponsor is a more significant relationship for you and your making things happen for yourself and your career than your mentor or boss. On the other hand, it's a less direct relationship, because you sometimes don't even know who they are! You can't pick them or assign them or ask them out to tea, per se. But you can certainly *cultivate* sponsors—and you must. You really need advocates for you, your skills, and abilities.

Eek! What Even *Is* a Sponsor?

A sponsor is an individual who is going to be pulling for you when you are not in the room. When he or she really knows and is impressed by you, they are able to advocate for you in big ways. A sponsor has the power, in your organization or field, to open doors for you, to clear a path to a new job or company or opportunity, and to influence people you likely don't yet have access to.

Jone Johnson Lewis puts it really clearly on *The BalanceCareers.com*: "A sponsor is someone with power who knows you and your potential, who advocates for your success on the corporate (or organizational) ladder, and who helps remove obstacles to your progress. A sponsor is someone who is willing to champion your progress.

"A sponsor is someone who has enough clout to make a difference in decisions others make about your progress. A sponsor believes in you and your skills and abilities enough to risk her or his own credibility for you.

"A sponsor has enough faith in your ultimate success to protect you so that you can take risks and make occasional mistakes and missteps without those setting your career back."[80]

Sponsors can be anyone in your company or even your field who has a direct experience of your great work: your skills (including all those core competencies cracked!), your excellent attitude, your focus and energy, and the contribution you make or will make to your current team and potential future position.

Some sponsors evolve from being mentors, after getting to know you through directly hearing from you, advising you, and experiencing your curiosity and relationship-building outreach. But the key to any sponsor taking on your cause is they have to check you out in action! A sponsor relationship can evolve from their seeing you operate within the company, on specific projects, or through work you do outside your immediate job.

Either way, a sponsor is someone who develops a vested interest in your success.

How to Attract Great Sponsors

Sure, your boss and immediate superiors can become terrific sponsors for you and your career: they have direct knowledge of your aptitude and contributions, strengths, and successes. So, continue making your boss look great! She'll notice and remember your efforts when someone asks for an internal recommendation to a new team or project. That's being a sponsor.

But you also want to take advantage of other opportunities to be seen, to be active, and to meet other people in your company who can vouch for you, as sponsors. People who can see you at your best, know about your successes, and even get to know your aspirations for the future.

This is another great benefit to joining one of your in-company Affinity Group or organization's ERGs. Each of these always has a senior person as an advisor, and more often than not this is someone who does not work directly with you, in your job. Another opportunity to seek out or volunteer for is cross-functional teams, where you join up to work with employees from other departments or divisions on a common project or goal.

By participating in these groups, particularly by volunteering to lead a project or help run a committee, you give senior management a great chance to check you out—and they *are* doing so, even if you don't know it! These are the sort of individuals who can vouch for you without your knowledge. They are people who often become aware of a new opportunity you might be right for in another department or maybe even outside the company.

A sponsor will put your name forward because they have seen what you do, they like what they see, and they don't mind attaching their name to your name.

So, to get noticed by potential sponsors, you need to volunteer for teams, projects, or cross-functional committees. And include volunteering for cross-functional projects or teams in different departments—say, if you're in accounting, jump on a project in operations to get to know those people and help advance a different sort of endeavor. Operating teams are very much in the center of the action, so they provide valuable experience as well as introductions to managers, if that's not your general work product or scope.

In ERGs or affinity groups, you can swiftly expand your exposure by volunteering to lead a project or committee. You'll then have opportunities to present, to brainstorm with top management, and to take on committees where you don't even have to apply your specific work-department skills. Even if you're in accounting, you don't have to be the treasurer on an Affinity Group board. You can be the chairperson!

You can get sponsors this way All Day Long. These are people you would not meet otherwise, and wouldn't work with or be seen by. But, in an ERG or Affinity Group, you can be noticed, you can show off, you can practice skills, and you can really build your sponsor network. Just be honest with senior executives who may become sponsors; they always have more seniority and professional capital, so you don't want to surprise them, if they put their credibility on the line to advocate for you. Be sure they know and see the real you and at your very best.

You may not even know who your best sponsors are, but their support for you will only increase as they see what you can do and how you do it.

###

STEP 7

TIME TO ENGAGE A COACH?

"Those who dream by day are cognizant of many things which escape those who dream only by night."

—Edgar Allan Poe

IT MAY BE TOO early in your career to contemplate (or pay for!) a professional coach. I haven't always had one, myself. Even after two decades in my career, engaging a professional coach is relatively new for me. But I can certainly say it is extremely beneficial, especially if you are mid-career or feel strongly you are stuck, maybe trying without success to change jobs, or considering a change in your field or career's direction.

This is not an inexpensive investment in yourself or your career, so it is a Step to take when you have some economic stability but need a deeper analysis of your career steps and résumé than a current mentor or sponsor can provide.

What Can a Career Coach Do?

Career coaches make job transitions, including applying and interviewing and negotiation for a new position, their expertise. They are attuned to HR trends and have current connections based on helping other job-seekers. Some are tied to specific industries or niches; their expertise is deep but targeted. Others are very useful even when you aren't changing jobs but want to do some strategic career analysis and planning.

Business News Daily interviewed some thought leaders at Jobvite, Monster, and ResumeCompanion.com about career coaches, asking them who are the best clients and how they can help you, in your career development.

The Chief People Officer at Jobvite, Rachel Bitte, calls career coaches a "brand-awareness team." She says, "'These professionals understand how to pinpoint the best aspects of your professional experience and market it in the most attractive way possible to potential employers. They're well-versed in crafting résumés, career planning, motivation techniques, and, most importantly, network building.'"[81]

Coaches are usually certified by one of a few credentialing organizations, like the National Career Development Association, NACE, the Academies, Career Directors International, and PARW/CC. Many have had careers in human resources or executive recruiting.

And there is a distinction made between "coaching," which "tends to be a solution-oriented approach that involves working with clients to see what concrete steps they can take to achieve career objectives," as opposed to "career counseling," which certified career coach and CareerFolk founder Donna Sweidan describes in *Forbes* as "more process driven—you look at whether there are any behavioral, emotional, or psychological issues that could be impeding a person's desired career ambitions."[82]

Sweidan adds, "But the core virtue of career coaching is to help people assess their professional situations with a greater degree of honesty, curiosity, empathy, and compassion."

Monster Career Expert and professional coach Vikki Salemi details the variety of ways coaches can help you, from looking at "long-term dream careers, what (clients) currently do, and how their next job can lead them closer to their dream job. ... Coaches also ensure accountability, to keep the job seeker on track and moving toward their next role."[83]

Should You Look into a Coach?

Getting professional input into your career path and prospects is often helpful. If you're this far into my book, you are serious about the professional development and skills advancement needed to excel in the workplace you're in, at the very least, allowing for progress both in your organization and your field. That way, your job really does become a satisfying, exciting career, and you can achieve your mission and vision for impacting the world.

If you're also ready to move to the next level or maybe pursue some new career path or passion, you can learn a lot from consulting with a trained professional.

Coach Vikki Salemi adds, "If you're thinking about leaving your job but aren't sure, you may want to hire a career coach. It's important to be proactive. Don't wait until it feels like you absolutely detest your job and can't stand going into the office."[84] And, of course, do your homework and figure out which coach or type of specialization will help you evaluate what you need to do next and how. They have different skill sets and priorities.

Having a career coach works for me because the woman I work with asks strategic questions about my situation, like, "Where do you want to go?" And "How do you want to get there?" She requires my answers to be pretty specific and she holds me accountable. She doesn't let me off the hook. She schedules a time by which I have agreed to do some thinking about an issue or some planning around an action step. My coach gives me homework, in other words! And I have to report in. Then she makes her suggestions. While we come to ideas and solutions together, effectively, she is an outside advisor who can really guide my direction or decisions. This works well for me.

You have to be ready to have a career coach. And in order for the investment and time to be effective, you have to be honest with yourself. This is not about hiring a cheerleader or someone to placate you. Those people have their place in our professional constellation. A career coach, however, is meant to be more challenging, and you have to be open to whatever suggestions they're going to make.

So, you will decide if you are ready to confront things and/or change your approach to your job or career, at this point. Look at a coach as a resource and then figure out if one would help you at this point in your career process, or maybe better in a year or two or even later.

Again, remember, this step involves some financial commitment on your part. But even still, it should be a big red flag if, after you do some research and get some recommendations, anyone you are considering working with asks for a big upfront fee.

Resume Companion career adviser Lauren McAdams says, "Always pay by the hour for a career consultant's time.

This ensures that you aren't locked into a potentially underwhelming service long-term and protects you from a fly-by-night operation.

We'll also continue to discover how you can build a network of mentors and advisors who can help get you feedback without going to this expense just yet. And please remember, when you revisit your own goals and mission statement then check in and monitor your own progress or changes, you are also going to "coach" your own career in the most perceptive way: by you, from the inside!

###

STEP 8

ESTABLISH A GROUP OF ADVISORS

"Risk more than others think is safe. Dream more than others think is practical."

—Howard Schultz, CEO of Starbucks

YOUR ADVISORS are going to be a group of people who know you. They can be internal and external, (i.e., work inside your same company or outside of it; be in your field or maybe be professionals in another realm altogether). What is important is this: when you bring them work-related situations, problems, questions, or decisions, they will tell you the truth.

You use these trusted people, advisors, for *advice*. You don't call a meeting of everyone when something comes up that you have to decide, do, change, or act on, however; you speak to them independently. But if you talk to four or five people about the same topic and get consistent feedback or recommendations, even if this response is not in alignment with what you were *thinking*, before asking, then you definitely should revisit your approach and look at it again!

Populate your group of advisors with people who both know you well *and* who have the experience to provide counsel to you. Again, you do not just have to draw advisors from within your company or even in your business or industry. "Outsiders" work just as well, and sometimes better.

Personally, I call my advisors a mastermind group. Mine is comprised of a number of people whom I can trust and talk to about work-related matters. I have known each of my advisors for a long time, so you may be looking at teachers or college colleagues as well as people you developed rapport with in your early jobs or mentorships to be part of your advisory team.

Now, because I have history and experience with my trusted advisors, I often know where they're coming from and what they may say, when I call to bounce ideas or strategy off them. But what is great about them, in my professional life, is sometimes they surprise me or throw me off. Those are some of the best situations for my growth, as a manager, because I can develop a new approach or change gears in order to be more effective, because my advisors opened my eyes to something I hadn't seen.

Who Should I Pick?

You want your advisors to be people you admire and respect. Otherwise, you won't take their advice or thought process seriously, and that wastes everyone's time. They can be your friend or colleague or classmate, no hard feelings. But to figure as an advisor to you, you want to select a group of people who have knowledge and perspective, so you can ask them the ropes and expect insight and perspective.

Your sponsors or even mentors are likely people you can't talk to about certain things, either because they don't know you that way or because some internal questions are too sensitive for a boss or supervisor to be a good sounding board. Your advisors, however, should be smart, qualified people who know you well and to whom you can talk about *all* things work-related. Sometimes they are just friends who also happen to be professionals and are willing and able to talk to you. The best thing is they know you and can be honest.

You want to be able to turn to them and get solid counsel about what you can do about most anything: applying for a new task, smoothing out a problem with a co-worker, approaching your boss on an issue—anything!

And you shouldn't feel you need to use your advisors as sounding boards only on things you have no ideas about. It's not a problem if you already know what *you* think you should do. But it is still a great idea to check in. I find, when I do that, oftentimes what I think I should do changes or iterates, based on what I hear from my advisors.

Don't Skip This Step

I have noticed some professionals, both employees and colleagues, who do not put together their own group of trusted advisors. They do not, as a matter of professional practice, have people they can talk to. They just fly by the seat of their pants.

That can be lonely and unwise. Why not make decisions with some insight or perspective? None of us can be attuned to every possibility or consider all sides of a matter without talking it out. Of course, you have your skills and knowledge and you're doing your job, making decisions every day, but I find, every month or so, something comes up where I can make a decision more effectively or just more confidently after talking it out with a few of those people I consider to be trusted advisors.

I *strongly* recommend you think this through and develop or reinforce relationships with a variety of folks you can call about an issue every now and then.

In my case, for example, I had a situation about someone who works for me who left the office without notifying or asking me when the building lost WiFi for the day. It was a frustrating situation for everyone who worked with me. Some of us even went across the street to our local town hall, logged on, and kept working. She did not join us, although I suggested it, nor did she wait until a certain hour in the afternoon to see if the situation resolved itself. She just went home, along with a few others.

I wasn't certain how to respond or reprimand this employee, whom I like very much both personally and professionally, although I had an initial thought, based on knowing the situation and the person involved. Before acting, though, I called up a handful of advisors and laid out what had happened. I tried to be as neutral and unbiased as possible in describing the situation, and then asked them what they thought I should do.

Because this employee had not told me she was going home and had left before the time I'd stipulated—others of us actually returned to the office at that time and discovered the Internet was back up and working!—it was an issue. I had to decide what to do about the insubordination but did not want to jam her up by writing her up to HR or anything.

I reached out to my advisors and talked through the options. They don't know the employee/staffer, but they do know me and they provided counsel. Then I made a decision, which was to ground her from a travel opportunity.

Some of my advisors confirmed my instinct as to how to respond, while some thought I should go the HR route. One thing they all suggested and I did follow through on was to talk through the incident with her. I listened to her rationale/excuses, which helped clear the air, even though I didn't need to do that. Bottom line: I communicated it was not acceptable to me, as her boss, for her to leave work after just a text exchange between us.

She got the message.

###

STEP 9

BE LIKABLE!

If people like you they will listen to you, but if they trust you, they'll do business with you.

–Zig Ziglar

DO I THINK THERE ARE some people who don't know this Step already?

I definitely do.

In my experience, I find many people in the workplace who believe, as long as they're doing their job, they're going to be good to go. But it's *not* enough. Definitely not enough if you want to excel at your job and truly make things happen for yourself and your career.

Being likable is extremely powerful. That is a fact. And it's a fun, easy skill to practice and implement.

On the flip side, if you're *not* likable and you're not already the boss or person calling shots, you're not going to get a lot of cooperation from people who don't *have* to help you out. And as we've discussed throughout, you benefit from many people supporting your projects and helping you do your job or raise your profile.

Of course, managers and coaches have been preaching this fundamental step since Dale Carnegie published his book, *How to Win Friends & Influence People,* back in the 1930s. And while some of those strategies are a bit out of date, the basics are still a good start!

Carnegie's 6 Ways to Make People Like You

1. **Become genuinely interested in other people.** "You can make more friends in two months by being interested in them than in two years by making them interested in you."[85] This came up in our discussion of active listening, but that's just a technique to express this point, about humanist interest and curiosity. It is

the key to any lasting friendship, not to mention likely everyone you work with is both interesting in their unique way *and* a candidate to be your friend!

2. **Smile.** This reflects a positive attitude and a warm reaction to friends, co-workers, bosses, colleagues, and clients. Even strangers! Project inner contentment and smile, which will make others around you feel great. (According to *Psychology Today,* also using an quick up-down flash of your eyebrows as people approach and a tilt of the head while listening—which exposes your carotid artery to a speaker's primitive but influential brain!—also signals you do not pose a threat, which means you are a friend![86]

3. **Remember that a person's name is, to that person, the sweetest and most important sound in any language.** "The average person is more interested in their own name than in all the other names in the world put together."[87] I know this is easier for some people than others, but it is still worth *working* on the skill of remembering people's names, even if you aren't perfect. It really helps people like you because

your recalling their name makes them feel seen, remembered, and respected.

Drake Bayer, when he was a writer at *Fast Company*, said to first keep in mind that "remembering is a skill to be cultivated" then he offered these "four quick techniques to help remember anyone's name:

- **Fully engage:** Don't divide your attention. Getting distracted is easy–instead, push aside random thoughts and focus on the fact that you're trying to get to know this person.
- **Repeat their name:** Engrave that name into your frontal lobe with repetition. Then say the name aloud twice: first to confirm you're saying it correctly, and second as a conversation-starter.
- **Make an association:** Associations–*mnemonic devices*, if you're being fancy–are tools of the memory-building trade. Use your natural goofiness to your advantage and make funny connections to names–they'll anchor your memory.

- **Conclude with their name:** Close the conversation by saying the person's name. It'll be validating for them–*aw, they remembered!*–and give you another chance to convince your neurons to fire that way again."[88]

4. **Be a good listener. Encourage others to talk about themselves.** We definitely covered this under core competencies, but here is an added benefit of listening closely and well. It's natural to understand how people appreciate your actually caring about what they have to say. In addition to their liking people who listen, you as a listener will learn how to relate to them better, even what and how to sell them and what they truly need. Likely, you'll even discover how you and they might work together.

5. **Talk in terms of the other person's interest.** This follows on active listening, because we can ask questions, send follow-up articles or emails, and share information about what others are interested in once we know that information. They like you because they

feel heard, important, and it helps them value you, in return.

6. **Make the other person feel important—and do it sincerely.** The golden rule is to treat other people how we would like to be treated. We love to feel important, and so does everyone else. If you can be sincere about appreciating other people, complimenting their skill or success and appreciating things they do or think, you will succeed in the Carnegie method and "win all the friends you could ever dream of."

More Hacks

People like you when you can help them. As a digital native who has grown up with tech savvy and facility, you have a killer app for building fans around your office.

As Kasey Sixt, Vice President of CKR Interactive, says, "Everyone is stretched and needs help. Opportunities are always there to pitch in. Generationally, (you) are digital natives. You can add a lot by really being helpful—that's part of what you bring to the party. Just by saying *nicely* to a colleague or boss, 'I am a digital native. This comes second-nature to me. How can I help you navigate something? How can I help you get up-to-date on something?' And by doing this, it's a win-win. You are helping someone with a skill you find easy, but another person, because they're not a digital native, wouldn't even have thought to do it that way." And they will remember you for your help, skill, and tact!

Think of the ways you can help others in the workplace navigate a technical challenge or apply new tools, but in a kind way. Most anyone would appreciate your saying, "You're doing it the hard way. I just learned this trick. I think it might work for you..."[89]

I know *I* would!

Aja Frost offered a few great hacks on *The Muse* to make you instantly more likable because she, too, agrees that being liked is important for your success.[90]

She suggests starting by asking *someone else* to do you a favor which, she says, may sound counterintuitive but, according to the *Huffington Post*, is proven to make that colleague or co-worker or client like you more.[91] It worked, way back, for Benjamin Franklin—it's even called the Ben

Franklin Effect in social psychology circles—and it's still a tried-and-true way for building rapport.

Using words like "sir" and "ma'am," "You're welcome," "How can I help?" and even "I believe in you," can create great impressions and help those you're speaking to like you even more, as they're getting to know you.[92]

You can also laugh at yourself—people definitely warm to a bit of self-deprecation, plus "showing vulnerability and a sense of humor make you more likable and approachable."[93] Think about radiating energy and good-humor, but also be "easily impressed, entertained, and interested." All of this goes to helping people like and enjoy being around you.

So do all the active listening techniques and interpersonal skills described in Step 4, "Crack your Core Competencies," especially the idea of asking people about things that are important to them. It doesn't have to be artificial, like Dale Carnegie may seem today—like studying someone's office pictures to initiate conversations or ordering the same thing as a colleague or client, when you go out to lunch—but when it's genuine, people like to be listened to and have you be genuinely interested in them.

The key is to show that you think of whomever you're talking to as a person, not just part of a work or customer/client equation. And, as I mentioned, likability and listening strategies *also* become part of your process to find out what people need and want, which is a key way to learn how to sell to them, while coming off as curious, attentive, and congenial.

Being likable is part of your holistic process of developing yourself for success.

###

STEP 10

UNDER-PROMISE, OVER-DELIVER, & ALWAYS *DO THE WORK*

"Always deliver more than expected."

—Larry Page, co-founder of Google

HERE'S ANOTHER STEP that may sound obvious, but you would be surprised how many employees and interns I observe who don't yet grasp how critical this is for their own success, and how much impact you can have, doing this right.

You have a work scope, usually defined by your boss, supervisor, team leader, or all of the above (sometimes at the same time!). It can be a lot, no matter where you are in the pecking order at your organization. Like I said earlier: everybody is stretched. In addition to that, everything the boss and company needs is important *and* probably was needed yesterday...

Yes, we're all dealing with this pressure at work. But my point is you have been hired by a certain boss or bosses, and hopefully you have a good job description. It can take a little while to really understand what all that entails and then a little longer to grasp how you can do everything well, efficiently, and effectively. But each of the Steps in this book should help you analyze what your work is and how to get it all done.

It is your responsibility to keep asking, watching, and learning so you *really* understand what the work is. And then to be sure, using everything you have and know, that you are doing the full job expected and needed of you. That is key!

How to Over-Deliver and Why

You will stand out if you do *more* than the work. Unfortunately, and not in a good way, you *also* stand out if you over-promise and under-deliver!

Over-delivering can mean going that extra mile on an assignment, including formatting or proofing a report before you submit the draft; getting things in just a day or few hours before you *have* to, to let your supervisor have a jump on it or know sooner that it's under control; showing up early to help set up an event or meeting, even if that's not your job; and staying late when the team is on deadline, even if it's not technically your hours—remember: someone always needs help—or after an event, to help clean up, organize materials, and assist speakers or upper managers.

Under-delivering is the opposite. In the workplace, it is particularly important, when you say you're going to do something, that you do it. Whatever it is.

And avoid over-promising. *Don't* say you're going to do five things for your boss on a certain project if you're not sure you can *deliver all five*. Your reputation, your brand,

and your ability to be effective in your team or department will be hurt any time you over-promise and under-deliver. If you do not complete the work scope you commit to by the deadline you or boss need it, it's just not good!

Much better is to *say* you'll definitely accomplish two of the five necessary tasks by the deadline and then work especially hard to deliver three or four... That's going the extra mile and will be noticed. You *know* all five are needed, but you don't want to over-promise if it's unrealistic you'll get them all done in the time requested.

The same goes for deadlines, because these are very important in business. Your boss and department leaders are carrying a lot of workflow and schedules around in their head, so when you make a commitment to get something done by a certain time and then do not make the date, it has a ripple effect of problems, often for more people than just you and your word.

Instead, if you're asked to do A+B+C by a certain date for someone, consider saying, "I can't promise all that by that particular date. Can we push the date back—I can do everything by such and such a date? Or I can do part of the work—say, A + B—by that date or sooner, and then tackle C."

And then, you most certainly can *try* to bring those parts in earlier or deliver more parts by the deadline! But you won't be caught offering what you can't deliver.

Take Ownership

One of Amazon's top leadership principles is **Ownership.** This is another way of demonstrating your commitment to really doing the work. How does your attitude measure up to that company's definition? (And remember: "leaders" applies to you at any stage of your career, whether you're leading your own work to make your boss look great, starting to lead teams or project groups in your organization, or putting yourself out there as a volunteer leader for an ERG or Affiliates group.) "Leaders are owners. They think long term and don't sacrifice long-term value for short-term results. They act on behalf of the entire company, beyond just their own team. They never say 'that's not my job.'"[94]

The young Amazon Web Services engineer Corey Salzer, who landed her job with the company right out of college, discussed this and other Amazon leadership principles in her initial job interview. She chose to include her understanding of how this applied even to taking ownership of her own internship projects and tutoring website, which she designed in college. "In my interviews, we talked about how I could scale that or how I would deal with different failure scenarios, so I was displaying a lot of ownership in that sense," Salzer said. She suggests you can start talking to employers, both prospective and current, in these same terms. For example, "I had ownership over this project, and I made X decisions that impacted Y. Those decisions benefitted the entire team/company."[95]

You Have to Put in the Time

The biggest anxiety I see in millennial workers, and something that is mentioned most by managers and bosses I meet, is their wanting everything—success, advancement, promotion, responsibility, the next opportunity—*now*, without putting in the time or waiting for it to happen.

It. Will. Happen! I guarantee. We all confirm that for you, as supervisors and bosses: it will happen for you, too, if you put in the time to develop your brand, crack your core competencies, develop the unique skills needed for your job and the one above you, and demonstrate you will consistently do the work, when asked, on time and well. That is when the rewards come, but not before.

Because of the technology with which you have grown up, so much of your life is quick and "right now"— information, connections, purchases, entertainment. Oftentimes you don't see or believe that the opportunities to advance or continue to grow really *are* coming.

It is fine to have expectations in your workplace: that you will be appreciated, that you will be promoted and advanced, if you put in the time, that your mentors and sponsors will watch out of for you and bring you in, so you feel like an effective and included part of the team.

What is problematic, however, as described by Kasey Sixt at CKR Interactive, is "the patience isn't there. The opportunities will appear if you stick it out! You have to get to know the organization and make your mark. You can't expect anything and shouldn't go in expecting that the world will be handed to you. However, if you lead with 'How can I provide value?', everything else will come.

"Especially on teams. You want to put in the time and focus on helping other people. In an organization, everyone has different talents and each one is needed, to have successful projects and programs and teams. Your focus should not be on 'when' but on using your talent, your contribution, and great work, to make everyone look good. That is what pays off."

She goes on to remind employees looking to excel, "If you have the attitude that everyone can win and you can help in some way, through your work, to make everyone look good, that may be your missing ingredient. Understand that *everyone* wins, *everyone* can be successful. *Your* success doesn't preclude (anyone else's) success."[96]

Hand-in-hand with patience is resilience. Part of putting in the time is recognizing your projects and jobs and careers are not usually linear. There are setbacks! But those can be hard on those of you for whom things comes easily and happen quickly.

I played tennis as a kid, so I knew from an early age that setbacks are part of the process. If you haven't had that experience yet, please be prepared. Develop resilience and resist fearing or failing to expect setbacks in the continuum of gaining experience and putting in time. Recognize, when they happen, you have to get back out there and make a course correction. You're still in charge of making it happen. Just see setbacks as inevitable, part of the natural progress and timing of jobs and careers.

In my experience, at every level, there are also employees who sort of want to just mail it in. *You can't.* Not at any stage of your career. You have to be proactive and patient, in order to progress and be successful—and to be most satisfied, honestly, because you're growing and being recognized.

The fact is the best performers in any field, sport, or discipline in the world don't just do the work. They do extra. They continue to iterate, put in the time, and over-deliver. That includes Roger Federer and Serena Williams. LeBron James and Stephen Curry. Beyoncé and Adele.

You can say, "Hey, I'm not on *that* level. What does that mean for me?"

Well, the point is, *even* people on that level keep doing the hard work, practicing, putting in time, refining what they do. So, all of us need to do it, too!

Remember that *Business Insider* podcast I mentioned, with John Sculley talking about Apple CEO Steve Jobs?[97] In it, he also reiterated how those natural, comfortable presentations Jobs did every year for shareholders and the tech press were far from off-the-cuff. Jobs *practiced* each one of those for many, many hours in order to *look* effortless while communicating complicated concepts with precision and clarity. Lots of practice. Changes and adjustments. More practice.

You, too, must expect to do all that's required, in order to get that next raise, promotion, or transfer. There are no shortcuts to this aspect of making progress in your career. All the great things will come to you by putting in the work, not just by showing up and being there…

In my current crop of twenty-seven USTA interns, only three of them went the extra mile this past summer and made the rounds to meet senior staff, cultivate sponsors and mentors, dive in to how our corporate culture works, and figure out what matters. The work product of everyone was just fine. But I know that those three interns will go on to be particularly successful because they are leveraging the opportunity to meet people, to gather advisors, and to be remembered.

Sometimes, in some work environments, you may not be exposed to the appropriate ways to put in the time in the way your managers were, when they started out in their careers. We have different technologies now and different management styles than fifteen, twenty years ago. People work remotely; some projects and departments are very siloed from colleagues or co-workers.

My observation is that many younger employees don't always see their managers and bosses and senior executives "putting in the time" in the way I'm talking about in this section. Maybe you're seeing your boss leave the office regularly at 5:36 p.m., so you assume you can, too! But you have not yet built all your relationships yet, haven't developed your brand, and haven't put in all the time your boss has. They are likely working remotely, taking important outside meetings or social events, and then putting in more hours at home after dinner.

I know the counter-energy to putting in more time is your impatience at having to wait for that promotion or that raise. When does *your* time commitment pay off, you wonder?

Well, it pays to ask for more responsibility. Of course, first you want to get done what you're supposed to get done, but then, see what more you can take on, from your boss or for your team. Put in *that* extra time.

Now, while I strongly encourage you to ask to do more but not necessarily with your hand out. We all want more money, but first get that additional responsibility. This is guaranteed to set you up in the future—and it could be the *near* future! By taking on more and putting in more time, you can easily start doing the job above you—and make it easy to promote you (with a raise)!

I do see some employees who will listen to this advice. But I am among many managers who supervise team members who are adamant they do not want to do anything extra, whether it's tasks or time, unless they are being paid or promoted. Please, take my advice: don't worry about getting paid for it right away. First, set yourself up.

And, overall, please don't assume you can cut corners on putting in the time. You can't. Not if you expect to get ahead and make things happen. Focus on delivering on your work and spend extra time doing it. That is what will get you noticed, selected, and relied upon.

And It Has to Be *Good!*

The work you deliver, in addition to the right quantity and timeliness, also has to be first-rate! Your boss and team and department really need your work product to be usable, as there's rarely time to correct or supplement what you're supposed to deliver, not to mention there's rarely anyone available to do it over!

So, make your considerations of quality part of your commitment not to overpromise. If you're not sure you can do something well, be sure to ask for lots of help and guidance the first few times. It's always fine to ask clarifying questions, like, "Not sure what you need here…"

Or, if you know you'll need a learning curve to tackle something, build that into your timetable for your promises on delivery times and dates.

Employees on your level aren't the only ones to suffer from overpromising. Many a manager and supervisor are caught or lose their job for promising what they thought *should* get done without knowing what they *could* attain. It suggests the manager doesn't really understand her organization or the players who will be responsible for helping deliver on her promises, when she misses the mark and overpromises. Knowing how to get things done in your organization, as we've been discussing throughout, is going to ensure you avoid this pitfall. It will help make your promises all that more accurate!

Making promises is important. You can't *not* make them—to your boss, your project, your supervisor, etc. But bring to bear all the Steps and skills we've discussed throughout this book to be sure you can deliver and ensure your personal work is good.

And protect yourself. If there are four steps to a job or components to a project you're handling, check in with your boss when you finish the better part of the first. Nothing is stopping you! Keep asking, "Does this work? Or should I go in another direction?" And, "I need your counsel—can you take a look at this?"

These are smart choices to ensure success for your delivering on your promises. Check in! Don't go too far down the rabbit hole in the wrong direction.

While you have to do the work and do it well, even if you think you *also* have to do it on your own, you don't! It's not a bother to your boss or department if you keep circling back and checking in. It's important to do, in fact. And this will really enhance your chances for success.

###

STEP 11

VOLUNTEER TO GAIN EXPERIENCE

"The best way to protect your future is to create it."

—Abraham Lincoln

YES, YOU HAD TO do community service in high school, most likely, or you likely volunteered for events or fundraisers as part of college groups or Greek houses.

This Step is different. You can leverage opportunities to volunteer, as a professional, because they tie directly to key skills-development and networking opportunities for your career. Volunteering can also help make happen important personal aspects of your mission and purposes, whether in tandem with your work and job or as a holistic add-on to the projects you pursue in the workplace.

In fact, it is often best to volunteer for something that is outside your particular job scope. So, say you're in accounting and finance, you can find plenty of ways to volunteer where you don't even have to bring those skills to bear. You are able to bring value to a cause or project by volunteering to do a variety of different things and, more important, the experience with be valuable to you.

As you volunteer for cross-functional teams or get involved with ERGs and Affinity Groups, you will be able to access professional development and networking opportunities. You will also naturally gain exposure to upper-level managers and senior staff, and you'll find opportunities to work on projects or in sectors you wouldn't normally cover, in the course of your daily work. Even better, you will often find easy opportunities to lead a project, program, or event, showing off your leadership skills, while being seen by people all across your organization.

Opportunities Inside Your Organization

Start by looking for opportunities to volunteer for projects and project-based cross-functional teams within your company. Every organization has them going on, whether in your department, as a representative of your department on a group project, or even for something interesting that is entirely outside of the scope of your department.

Next, research all of the affinity groups or ERGs (employee resource groups) that your organization has and see which ones apply to you and are doing projects or collaborations that interest you. I can tell you *this* is a secret sauce to success for so many reasons: you will receive professional development, as that's the nature of these associations; there will always be networking opportunities with others in your company, community, and field; you will have exposure to executives other than your boss, because senior management is always assigned to affinity groups and ERGs, as supervisors and liaisons; and you'll find plenty of opportunities to work on volunteer projects, which you can quickly rise to lead. This is what you want to do!

Yes, often there is a social component to these groups, but that's not your focus. In fact, more and more ERGs are positioned by the company or association management to focus on key issues that matter to the organization. Oftentimes, senior leadership identifies, say, six or seven key areas of concern to the company and its various business units. Then, the Affinity Group or ERG chooses one to three of those areas to focus their meetings and activities around. The most purposeful groups are involved in problem-solving for the organization, which gives them more juice than those that operate as mere social networks.

Remember: if you can put yourself in a leadership position at one of your company's Employee Resource Groups (we call them Business Resource Groups at the USTA, and we have seven to choose from: a women's organization; young professionals; ACE (African-American/Caribbean); Hispanic-Latinx; Asian-American; working parents; and LGBT and partners), you will have immediate and natural access to top management. This is just exactly what you've been working on throughout the Steps in this book: for mentoring, for nailing your company culture and how things are done; for being noticed by the people who matter in your organization; for developing sponsors and advisors at the highest levels of your organization and outside your own business group.

Oftentimes, being a leader in these groups will give you a platform to present or for show-and-tell on some topic or program or plan. These days, most every company and organization has a variety of groups like this. In my experience, oftentimes employees at the lower levels of an organization don't always join—but there is *nothing* stopping you from participating and then reaping all these benefits. Don't be shy! Dive in! Just raise your hand and take on a leadership position.

You will get exposure outside what you usually do, which means your skills and work are seen by a different set of eyes than usual. Remember: in your company, people are always watching! So, while you are taking advantage of these chances for exposure and professional development of new skills, this Step often plays out in a very positive way for those who take advantage of it.

External Opportunities

Take stock first of your company culture and its giving priorities and community engagement. Kasey Sixt of CKR Interactive advises, "Look at your company. If they do a lot around giving back, if they make a concerted effort toward corporate giving and volunteering in the community or around core causes, as is generally now part of every corporate culture, they will want 100% employee participation." So, see where your company leadership is giving and volunteering.

Then look at where you, personally, really want to participate. This falls on your work-life continuum: they tend to blend more for you than be two separate silos of time and experience. Connect back to your mission and purpose, and then find where you can volunteer while providing the most value.

As CKR's Kasey Sixt adds, "If you come in asking, where am I going to provide the best value, you'll find the right niches. You can find value and bring back to your company. And the more you participate, the more you'll get back. *Be All In*. Then you'll find lots of opportunities."[98]

In addition to volunteering for events and such, in your community and/or company, also look at local non-profit organizations or local branches of a national non-profit that has a mission and values to help bring about change that resonates with you. Use your volunteer time for your humanistic soul development and your engagement with the community where you live, in order to give back and/or change or fix things. You will be able to find volunteer opportunities that align with your priorities as well as support what your city or neighborhood needs. And again, these don't have to be in the same field as your job. You can work in sports or media or tech or pharma and then volunteer in homeless services or food security, animal welfare or tutoring under-privileged kids—whatever you love! And wherever you can bring value.

In addition to generally helping these non-profits deliver their great work through your time and energy, also volunteer for a committee and then for their Board of Directors. Again, everyone needs help, and your leadership experience and networking opportunities will expand exponentially, when you do this.

Think about volunteering for positions where you can use or develop skills you'd like to gain, in addition to what you know/in the areas you're working already. So, for example, volunteer as treasurer or lead with your accounting skills on the finance committee or marketing experience for an event or PR committee, but also pick ways to get experience in event management, in fundraising, or in community outreach, if those aren't part of your professional training or daily work.

Not only can you develop new skills through these volunteer opportunities, you can also build your network in creative ways. Plus, you'll have a different sort of thing to add to your résumé.

###

STEP 12

NETWORK

"Our prime purpose in this life is to help others. And if you can't help them, at least don't hurt them.

—Dalai Lama

NETWORKING, IN ORDER to grow your connections and expose you to more people and resources in your field, is still very important! But there are great new ways to do it that will amplify your impact and serve your career. It's not just about going to events and seeing how many business cards you can collect!

Like *Harvard Business Review's* readers, you might hate networking. The HBR writers of "Learn to Love Networking" certainly hear this all the time, from students to executives to professionals new and seasoned—that it's uncomfortable, feels unnatural, maybe a little sleazy!⁹⁹ Of course, some of you are natural extroverts who flourish in social environments, but even if you're not, this Step is about understanding why networking is necessary and then it gives you great ways to network that will help you and your career.

What's the Objective?

LinkedIn helps by explaining, "Networking becomes a little clearer if we give it a different name: professional relationship building. It's all about getting out there (both on and offline), meeting people who work in your profession or your industry, and building a relationship with them. The goal of networking is to create a professional network. That means a group of professional contacts you know well enough to call in a favor from and for whom you wouldn't object doing a favor. It's as simple as that."¹⁰⁰

Simple but important. Important why? Well, because it's going to help you do your job, build your career, and be more effective at all of it!

Harvard Business Review cites lots of research that links the professional networks you develop to "more job and business opportunities, broader and deeper knowledge, improved capacity to innovate, faster advancement, and greater status and authority ... Plus, building and nurturing professional relationships also improves the quality of work and increases job satisfaction."[101] In other words: networking is connected to key ways to make things happen for you and your professional life.

First, you need to recognize you are looking for something different out of the two types of professional networks you can build, as described in *Forbes*. First, there's your **Expansive** network, which is a "broad umbrella group of contacts, ... present and former colleagues plus industry contacts, who can either speak specifically to your work experience and accomplishments or offer a broader personal endorsement of you as a potential hire." You network to meet and get to know colleagues, competitors, and maybe even mentors because these are "people who can connect you with potential jobs opportunities, ...

including family members or friends who can help you steer your job search in the right direction."[102]

The second is called a **Nodal** network, which you build through what *Forbes* calls "street-smart networking." This is a "more narrow subset of people, but also a more powerful group of 'marquee' contacts, who may wield influence in your industry or with hiring managers and other leaders who make hiring decision." You develop relationships with these network members over time so they can use their influence—as sponsors and recommendations—to "speak to your talents, experience, and character."[103]

You should also think about building up the following subcategories of networks, which may sometimes overlap with your big two. This list can help you refine your objectives—like who you'd like to meet or why you'd like attend a conference, in order to hear and meet with some of these types of people or connect with them on social media, etc.:

1. **Operational networks**[104]: These may be people in your particular field or members of professional organizations you join. They know about your sort of

work and what it takes to do it well, so that is how they would come to know and value you and your accomplishments.

2. **Strategic networks**[105]: These are thought-leaders, visionaries; people you admire or follow or read first, perhaps, and then seek out or get to know. They are very helpful for career planning or direction-changing; they can advise you on seeing the big picture around what you hope to accomplish and how you are going about it, with your goals and networking and skills development.

3. **Personal networks**[106]: These are people you meet through a variety of encounters, histories, or activities, starting with your school alums but also social media connects and those whom you meet in meet-ups or at other network-building events.

Start to shift your orientation to networking so you can see it as a learning experience, something that supports your mission and goals, rather than a duty or a negative obligation. Evaluate opportunities to attend conferences, mixers, meet-ups, coffees, etc., in terms of how they can connect with your personal "growth, advancement, and the accomplishments networking can bring." Then, when you're at any work-related social function, be curious; approach these events with an open mind, in order to get the most out of your time and investment.[107]

What else is great about networking? Well... you might find a mentor, if you "network in the right places... Chances are that you'll meet a lot of experienced professionals and experts in your sector. If you're at the beginning of your career, getting tips and insights from those who've been there and done it all before can be priceless."[108]

You might hear about a job, project, or opportunity at networking events that isn't yet advertised or hasn't been made public. Or, if you're thinking about a position in a different town or company, you may meet someone you can ask about that. "If you want to be in with a chance of getting that sought-after internal promotion or of moving to a more interesting or challenging role with a new company, you'll need to network to find out about them." Remember, people recommend people they know and like, so, "even if you're not networking directly with a group directly responsible for hiring, there's still a good chance that someone in your network will have the opportunity to make a recommendation."[109]

You'll definitely learn more about your field, the industry you work in, and your professional landscape with all its ups and downs when you get out and meet people who share your professional sector. Oftentimes, networking events are where you can effortlessly find out about who's going where or what companies are changing hands and other significant developments, not to mention you will get natural exposure to new ideas and points of view. This education and new input can help you not just in changing jobs but in doing your current job better.

If you continue to feel ambivalent about diving in and attending those functions or committing to do active networking, consider revisiting your mission and goals, the things *you* want to accomplish personally and professionally. The *HBR* authors reiterate, "Any work activity becomes more attractive when it's linked to a higher goal. So, frame your networking in those terms. We've seen this approach help female executives overcome their discomfort about pursuing relationships with journalists and publicists. When we remind them that women's voices are underrepresented in business and that the media attention that would result from their building stronger networks might help counter gender bias, their deep-seated reluctance often subsides."[110]

How to Hack Your Networking

First, **build your list of networking opportunities** so you have lots of choices and don't feel pressured to attend every event or conference or meet-up in your field. You also won't feel like you have a paucity of options for getting out there and working on this particular Step, in order to get things happening in your career.

To start, there are professional networking meetups in most every town, city, and industry. From Toastmasters (referenced earlier) to meetups for creative professionals, young professionals, remote workers, technology and business brainstorms, or just beers and business cards for making new local professional connections.

There are also local and regional organizations or branches of national organizations in most every city related either to professionals in your field or to your volunteer and/or social-change priorities. Search them out online or ask friends and colleagues for ideas about getting out and meeting folk from other companies but doing similar things.

These days, you can find a convention, conference, seminar, workshop, or professional gathering most every weekend, sometimes near and sometimes far. Some of these may be high-cost but perhaps high-value; other times, they may be more regional but perhaps with a speaker, sponsor, or mentor who intrigues you.

As Kasey Sixt of CKR Interactive recommends, seek out the organizations and networks "that give back to you— explore and discover those conferences, those associations. (Not to mention) there are webinars and so much content available on any subject and many professionals with words of wisdom. Try following them and figure out whether the speaker, podcaster, or teacher is speaking at a conference near you. Maybe you attend not for the conference but to connect with someone you follow on social media. Don't just choose from the predominant ones you think are best for your career. Pick ones that serve you better."[111]

Be strategic about where you spend your networking time and who you want to meet or learn more about. For the events you do attend, be active: don't just go to the workshop or keynote and leave; hang out at the social events, receptions, and the coffee breaks, where you can talk to people or ask follow-up questions.

Then, try to **deep-dive the connections you make**. Let's say you meet someone at a conference and exchange cards. First, try to keep in touch. Email the following week and then maybe quarterly or twice a year. Send a connection request through LinkedIn and study some of their associates and connections there. If you see an article that may interest her or him, reach out to them and send it along, in print or email, with a note that helps keep you on their mind and connects you with being helpful and perceptive. This is how to leverage your growing network and build relationships out of initial contacts or meet-ups.

Especially early in your career, seek out those conferences and workshops where you can learn new things, explore your field, and constantly meet new people.

And you don't have to do all the going-out to be an effective networker. You can **host your own event,** a great alternative way to build and nurture your network plus help other people expand their own connections. On the personal branding hub Reachcc.com, branding guru William Arruda encourages you to think about hosting anything from "a random event at your house or a recurring event at a chosen meeting place. This will provide an informal way to get together and connect the members of your network with each other. If each member brings a member of their network, it will also help to significantly expand yours."[112]

Next, **don't forget about your social networks**, which have become much more highly professionalized and valuable. LinkedIn, of course, positions itself as the leader in professional network-building and connections. Their Director of Executive Partnerships and key Pulse contributor Jordan Parikh reminds you, "If you have a great chat with someone at, for example, an event, don't be afraid to ask to exchange contact details or to connect on LinkedIn and to ask if you can follow up with them later."[113]

She also encourages you to join LinkedIn groups in your field or industry, sign up for long-form posts written by experts of interest, and "watch for specialist professional forums (often hosted by professional bodies), where you can ask and answer work-related questions."[114]

LinkedIn and other professional social networks make your network-building easier, helping you see connections and reach out to contact people through introductions from friends and colleagues. Just don't let this ease fool you: your purely online connection is not going to be particularly strong immediately. But it can be a great tool to help you strategize who you want to meet face-to-face, how to read up on and follow key voices and influencers in your field, and where to focus you networking event time and energy.[115]

LinkedIn is also organizing itself as a resource for networking and career-track development for the workplace, so check out what they're offering in their learning modules, as part of your social network cultivation. (*See Linkedin.com/learning.*)

Approach your networking events with a clear awareness of how you add value and what you can contribute. So, as *Forbes* writer Bonnie Marcus writes, **"understand your value proposition,** because it positions you as credible and helps you build influence, as well as create mutually beneficial relationships, because you understand how you can help others."[116] We have talked throughout this book about helping others—your colleagues, your teams, making your boss look good; serving and uplifting your community, as your mission and values. When you think of networking in terms of bringing value and finding ways to help those you meet, it won't feel so self-serving.

In truth, networking is about building connections and networks that benefit all members and sides. To "**build mutually beneficial relationships,**" bring your curiosity and active listening. "As you meet people, ask them open-ended questions about their work. What are they working on? What are some of their current challenges? Is there an opportunity for you to help, by connecting them to a resource or to guide them, based on your value proposition and/or experience? This is how you create strong relationships."[117]

To take this a step further, consider Taylor Insight Worldwide's CEO, André Taylor's recommendation about networking and building a meaningful professional network based on mutual support: "Find a group of people you can love. That is a far better approach to what people think of as networking than anything else. Think of them as extended family. Love them without the feeling you're trying to get something out of them. Now, don't be reluctant to ask for help, as you would from extended family, but first demonstrate how can you help them. Then think through how they can help you in ways that also help them...

"There is psychic value in helping. The long-term value in helping will surface. It will be there. This goes back to the idea I mentioned earlier about looking at a long-term professional horizon."[118]

You know your goals and interests. Use your networking to find people whose priorities align with yours and then think about how you can grow mutually beneficial working relationships. Northwestern University's Brian Uzzi calls this the **shared activities principle**. "Potent networks are not forged through casual interactions but through relatively high-stakes activities that connect you with diverse others," he explains.[119]

In "Learn to Love Networking," *HBR* goes on to add, "When your networking is driven by substantive, shared interests you've identified through serious research, it will feel more authentic and meaningful and is more likely to lead to relationships that have those qualities, too."[120]

And never underestimate *your* capacity to have value to offer someone you meet or want to connect with. For newer members of the workforce, this can be a problem, so please look at it head-on right here. *HBR* writes, based on reviewing a number of workplace studies, "We've found that people who feel powerless—because they are junior in their organizations, because they belong to a minority, or for other reasons—often believe they have too little to give and are therefore the least likely to engage in networking, even though they're the ones who will probably derive the most benefit from it."[121]

You have more to offer, however, than you realize. Allan Cohen and David Bradford, in their book *Influence without Authority*, write, "most people tend to think too narrowly about the resources they have that others might value. They focus on tangible, task-related things such as money, social connections, technical support, and information, while ignoring less obvious assets such as gratitude, recognition, and enhanced reputation. For instance, although mentors typically like helping others, they tend to enjoy it all the more when they are thanked for their assistance. The more heartfelt the expression of gratitude, the greater its value to the recipient."[122]

So, you can always start with appreciation for a senior person's connection, support, information, and guidance. Helping a mentor or sponsor look good in your circles has benefits similar to your making your boss look good.

Then remember, "you might also have unique insights or knowledge that could be useful to those with whom you're networking. For example," as we were discussing earlier about leveraging your digital native capabilities, "junior people are often better informed than their senior colleagues about generational trends and new markets and technologies."[123]

When you lead with helping rather than promoting yourself, you'll be more successful and feel better about networking. Not to mention it'll be more fruitful.

###

PART 3

Pull It Together

CONCLUSION

"Success is not attained by chance, you have to work in order to get it."

—Oscar Auliq-Ice

I GIVE YOU these Steps, competencies, and insights into crafting your vision and living your mission because, together, they have helped me and many top-level executives become successful and satisfied in our professional endeavors. This set of best-practices and proven strategies have supported and guided me as I figured out how to *Make it Happen* in my life. And I want you to succeed, too, while loving your chosen career!

I learned most everything here from my first bosses, jobs, mentors, and sponsors. But learning doesn't stop here. I still gather advice and professional development guidance from a professional coach regularly, and I consult my group of advisors on some work decision or direction every few weeks. I reconfirm my values and mission statement each New Year's, set new goals and benchmarks for the year, and check-in with them on a regular basis. And yes, even though I am many decades into my career and at a very senior level in my association, I still keep my eye on making my boss look good and advancing the mission and vision of my organization through the decisions I make and the way I get things done.

I invite you to gauge how you are doing on each of these Steps in your own life and career, and I hope you'll do a candid assessment of your core competencies from Step 4. I've quoted from a lot of smart thought leaders and advisors throughout the book and invite you to follow up with their wisdom and advice. And there are some excellent resources on the next page, notably blogs you can dip in on or read thoroughly as ways to continue your path to *Make it Happen.*

I wish you every success—even though, yes, as social investor and innovator Auliq-Ice says, you do have to work at it!

###

RESOURCES

"Be the change you want to see happen."

—Arleen Lorrance

- *The Muse.com:* The beloved and trusted resource for crafting fulfilling careers.
- *Medium.com:* Taps into the brains of the world's most insightful writers, thinkers, and storytellers to bring you the smartest takes on topics that matter.
- *LinkedIn.com/learning:* Learn business, creative, and technology skills to achieve your personal and professional goals. Join for access to thousands of courses.
- *TheOtherFiftyPercent.com:* blog and podcast network featuring voices from the other half of society.

And from Susie Moore at *TheMuse.com*, six great podcasts to stimulate your thinking and motivate your career[124]:

- *The James Altucher Show*

  Start With: Episode 36, "Ramit Sethi—What Does it Mean to Have a Really Rich Life?"

- *The School of Greatness* with Lewis Howes

  Start With: "The 10 Success Principles to Create Abundance with Jack Canfield."

- *The Charged Life* with Brendon Burchard

  Start With: "How Incredibly Successful People Think."

- *Tara Brach*

  Start With: "Real But Not True."

- *This Is Your Life* with Michael Hyatt

  Start With: "Season 5, Episode 5—How to Finally Achieve Work-Life Balance."

- *Being Boss* with Emily Thompson and Kathleen Shannon.

  Start With: "#42 Brene Brown."

###

ACKNOWLEDGMENTS

MY GREATEST debt of gratitude goes to my own mentors, sponsors, and teachers, who have taught and guided me along my own professional path, plus the coaches and colleagues who continue to advise and inspire me. In particular, thank you to all the Diversity and Inclusion thought leaders and professionals, my tribe, who help me and all our organizations excel by doing good.

This includes my personal Board of Advisors: my wife, Shelia D. Abrams; lifelong friends Derrick L. Alford, Jim Phipps, and Greg Williams; Aurora Austriaco; my sisters Diane Abrams and Bernadette Abrams-Torrance; Jared Bartie, Gloria Blackman, Donna Dozier Gordon, Chris Handy, Michael Kennedy, Bill Leong, Linda Mann, Rochelle Taylor, Renee Tirado, Henry M. Williams, and Michelle Blake Wilson.

I owe special thanks to André Taylor, Kasey Sixt, and the writers and editors at *The Muse* and *LinkedIn Learning,* for offering so much insight into this millennial workforce and the best ways to help them realize all their passion and potential. And to my early readers and advisors on this important subject, busy professionals who generously join me in bringing leadership and mentoring to the next generation: Dale Caldwell, Brian Wong, Bob Davis, Pamela A. McElvane, Jane Hyun, Jennifer Brown, Fabian J. De Rosario, Michon Ellis, and Ralph Moore.

###

ABOUT D.A. ABRAMS

D.A. (DAVID ANTHONY) ABRAMS is an author, speaker, coach, and advisor who currently serves as the Chief Diversity & Inclusion Officer for the United States Tennis Association (USTA) in Orlando, Florida, a position he assumed in February 2012. There, he focuses on developing and innovating the USTA's D&I initiatives on the national, regional, and grass-roots levels.

As a best-selling author and Certified Association Executive (CAE), Abrams utilizes a six-prong approach, while advocating D&I as one of the USTA's core values. The Association continues to embrace the D&I Strategic Approach to diversifying tennis for the good of the sport, which Abrams launched six years ago.

Currently, the USTA is operating under the third iteration of the "All Hands on Deck - Plan of Attack." A major component of the plan is the "Cross Cultural Dexterity Training" program, which serves to uncover unconscious bias, increase understanding of the negative impact of exclusionary behavior, and the power of intentional inclusion. He also developed a company-wide scorecard to measure the achievements of the USTA's D&I objectives, as well as identify "Areas of Opportunity." In 2013, Abrams launched a company-wide internship program. The program was implemented to provide diverse college-age students the opportunity to live the USTA experience for eight weeks.

He is also responsible for overseeing and cultivating the USTA's 7 Business Resource Groups (BRGs). Under his leadership, the USTA has made significant contributions to the business of the organization, including enhanced partner benefits and a greater parental leave policy for both mothers and fathers. Since his appointment as CDIO, the USTA has heightened its Supplier Diversity efforts, with year-end spend with diverse suppliers surpassing 16%; developed 7 D&I Engagement Guides supported by an Engaging Diverse Markets: An Application Toolkit.

Abrams oversees and operates the D&I training for all USTA Board of Directors, Council Chairs, Committee Chairs, C-Suite, USTA Staff, as well as the Presidents, Delegates and Executive Directors of all 17 USTA Sections. He serves as a member of the Diversity & Inclusion Committee, Hispanic Engagement Advisory Committee, and is chair of the D&I Advisory Group at the USTA. All serve to implement positive cultural change and address various areas of opportunity within the organization. In addition, Abrams is the chair of the USTA's Accreditation Review Committee. External to the USTA, he is the chair of the Diversity & Inclusion Sports Consortium, and board treasurer of the National Association of Asian American Professionals.

Abrams has been involved professionally in tennis since 1989 and has worked with the USTA in various capacities since 1993. In 1997, he became the first African-American to serve as the executive director of a regional/sectional office, assuming the post for the USTA Missouri Valley Section. After returning to the national office in 2000, he was hired as the executive director of USTA Eastern in 2006, making him the first person ever to pilot two different USTA sections. In 2000, he was named one of Tennis Industry Magazine's "Top 40 under 40" tennis executives. And in 2017, he was inducted into the USTA Middle States Section Hall of Fame.

Abrams has authored five other books: *Certified Association Executive Exam: Strategies for Study & Success* (May 2013); *Diversity & Inclusion: The Big Six Formula for Success* (July 2013); *New-School Leadership: Making a Difference in the 21st Century* (July 2014); *Association Management Excellence: Become an Expert by preparing for the CAE Exam* (October 2014); *The Inclusion Solution: My Big Six Formula for Success* (October 2016). *Make it Happen* (February 2019) is his sixth.

ABOUT THE AUTHOR

In 2012, *Sports Business Journal* highlighted Abrams in their "Executive Transactions" section and *Savoy Magazine* featured him and the USTA in its "Corporate Diversity Matters" section. In addition, he's been featured on the covers of *Associations Now Magazine* (July 2012) and *Diversity Executive Magazine* (August 2013).

At age twelve, D.A. was introduced to tennis via the National Junior Tennis & Learning program operating at Mander Playground located in the North Philly section of Philadelphia, Pennsylvania. The program served as a gateway to many life changing opportunities. He became a nationally ranked junior player, and played tennis at Millersville University in Pennsylvania where he earned his undergraduate degree in business administration, concentration – accounting (at no cost to his parents). Subsequently, Abrams earned a master's degree from Metropolitan State University in Minneapolis, MN, and continues to learn by way of reading, writing, and travel.

Abrams has been involved in tennis since being introduced to the sport via the National Junior Tennis & Learning program (NJTL) of Philadelphia. As a junior player, he excelled, earning national rankings in the United States Tennis Association, and the American Tennis Association. Good grades along with his hard work on the tennis court earned him a tennis scholarship to attend Millersville University of Pennsylvania. After graduation, he put his accounting degree to good use at Control Data Corporation based in Minneapolis, Minnesota.

Missing tennis, Abrams returned to Philadelphia after four years in the Twin Cities to serve as the Recruitment Director and Head Tennis Professional at the Arthur Ashe Youth Tennis Center (AATYC). While at AAYTC, he launched Dave Abrams Tennis Services, a full-service tennis company that offered tennis instruction to adults and juniors, as well as International Tennis Tours. Abrams has been a certified member of the United States Professional Tennis Association, and Professional Tennis Registry since the early 1990s.

In 1993, Abrams moved to White Plains to join the United States Tennis Association (USTA), where he is now Chief Diversity & Inclusion Officer and moved to their new Orlando headquarters in summer 2016. He has also served in the following capacities: Executive Director of two USTA Sections (Eastern, 2006-2012) and Missouri Valley (1997-2000); Director of Community Outreach (2000-2006); and National Coordinator, NJTL & Minority Participation (1993-1996).

As a board member of the Alzheimer's Association-Hudson/Rockland/Westchester, NY Chapter (July 2009 to June 2013), Abrams served in the following roles: Chair, Audit Committee; Member, Compensation Committee; Member, Nominating Committee; and Member, Development Committee. In addition, he played an active role in the New York Society of Association Executives (NYSAE; 2010-2011) as a member of the Membership and Education Committees and is a Current Member of the National Association of Asian American Professionals (NAAAP). It should be noted that Abrams is a Certified Association Executive (CAE).

Please feel free to connect with Abrams:

Via email: DAAbrams21@gmail.com

LinkedIn: LinkedIn.com/in/DAAbrams1

Twitter: @DAAbrams1

###

ENDNOTES

---

[1] Taylor, André interview. *www.AndreTaylor.com* 28 Aug 2018.

[2] Rowe, Stan. *www.Edwards.com.* 22 June 2017.

[3] Taylor, André interview. *www.AndreTaylor.com* 28 Aug 2018.

[4] Smith, Glenn. "7 Reasons Your Company Needs a Clear, Written Mission Statement." *GlennSmithCoaching.com.* 29 Mar 2016.

[5] Cantin, Marie. "Marie Cantin, Producer and Educator." *The Other Fifty Percent Blog, Episode 117:* Julie Harris Walker, producer. 12 Aug 2018.

[6] Keiser, Amelia. "How to Write a Personal Mission Statement (With Examples." *www.BrandYourself.com.* 11 June 2018.

[7] Cantin, Marie. "Marie Cantin, Producer and Educator." *The Other Fifty Percent Blog, Episode 117:* Julie Harris Walker, producer. 12 Aug 2018.

[8] Keiser, Amelia. "How to Write a Personal Mission Statement (With Examples." *www.BrandYourself.com.* 11 June 2018.

[9] Swartz, Mark. "Do You Have a Personal Mission, Vision and Values Statements?" *www.Monster.ca/career-advice*

[10] Davenport, Barrie. "How to Write a Personal Mission Statement in 8 Steps." *www.liveboldandbloom.com.*

[11] Sussex, Tatyana and Madsen, Susanne. "How to Create a Personal Mission and Vision Statement for Your Career." *www.LiquidPlanner.com* 25 Aug 2015.

[12] Steinberg, Amanda. "Meet our Founder Amanda Steinberg." *www.dailyworth.com*.

[13] Hendricks, Drew. "Personal Mission Statement Of 13 CEOs And Lessons You Need To Learn." *www.Forbes.com*. 10 Nov 2014.

[14] Covey, Stephen R. *The 7 Habits of Highly Effective People*. New York: Simon & Shuster, 1989.

[15] Keiser, Amelia. "How to Write a Personal Mission Statement (With Examples." *www.BrandYourself.com*. 11 June 2018.

[16] Davenport, Barrie. "How to Write a Personal Mission Statement in 8 Steps." *www.liveboldandbloom.com*.

[17] Davenport, Barrie. "How to Write a Personal Mission Statement in 8 Steps." *www.liveboldandbloom.com*.

[18] Hull, Patrick. "3 Tips for a Resolution You'll Keep Your Personal Mission Statement." *Forbes.com*. 27 Dec 2012.

[19] Hull, Patrick. "Answer 4 Questions to Get a Great Mission Statement." *Forbes.com* 10 Jan 2013.

[20] Feliciano, Dan. "Why are Goals and Objectives Important." *Fast Company*. 9 Apr 2008.

[21] Feliciano, Dan. "Why are Goals and Objectives Important." *Fast Company*. 9 Apr 2008.

[22] "Personal Branding Quotes: Powerful Advice you Can't Miss. "*BrandYourself.com*. 29 June 2018.

[23] Harris Interactive. *Just Google Me*. National Harris Study for BrandYourself. January 2013.

[24] "Skidmore career development course hits national airwaves." Skidmore News & Events. 26 July 2018.

[25] Feldman, Barry and Price, Seth. *The Road to Recognition: The A-to-Z Guide to Personal Branding for Accelerating Your Professional Success in The Age of Digital Media*. Washington, DC: IdeaPress Publishing. 9 May 2017.

26 "Number of Employers Using Social Media to Screen Candidates Has Increased 500 Percent over the Last Decade." *www.CareerBuilder.com/AboutUs*. 28 Apr 2016.

27 "Personal Branding Quotes: Powerful Advice you Can't Miss. "*BrandYourself.com*. 29 June 2018.

28 *Online Reputation in a Connected World*. Cross-Tab Marketing Research 2010 for Microsoft Corporation.

29 *Online Reputation in a Connected World*. Cross-Tab Marketing Research 2010 for Microsoft Corporation.

30 Keiser, Amelia. "How to Write a Personal Mission Statement (With Examples." *www.BrandYourself.com*. 11 June 2018.

31 Kalish, Alyse. "The 9 Rules of Being an Adult at Work." *www.The Muse.com/Advice*. 11 Apr 2018.

32 Kalish, Alyse. "The 9 Rules of Being an Adult at Work." *www.The Muse.com/Advice*. 11 Apr 2018.

33 Doyle, Alison. "Understanding Company Culture." *www.TheBalanceCareer.com*. 23 Aug 2018.

34 Wright, Casey. "10 Things to Know about Google's Awesome Culture." *The Huffington Post*. 2 May 2017.

35 Manjoo, Farhad. "The Happiness Machine: How Google Became Such a Great Place to Work." *Slate.com*. Jan 2013.

36 Wright, Casey. "10 Things to Know about Google's Awesome Culture." *The Huffington Post*. 2 May 2017.

37 Church, Alan H. and Conger, Jay A. "When You Start a New Job, Pay Attention to These 5 Aspects of Company Culture." *Harvard Business Review*. 29 Mar 2018.

38 Church, Alan H. and Conger, Jay A. "When You Start a New Job, Pay Attention to These 5 Aspects of Company Culture." *Harvard Business Review*. 29 Mar 2018.

39 Church, Alan H. and Conger, Jay A. "When You Start a New Job, Pay Attention to These 5 Aspects of Company Culture." *Harvard Business Review*. 29 Mar 2018.

[40] Church, Alan H. and Conger, Jay A. "When You Start a New Job, Pay Attention to These 5 Aspects of Company Culture." *Harvard Business Review*. 29 Mar 2018.

[41] Church, Alan H. and Conger, Jay A. "When You Start a New Job, Pay Attention to These 5 Aspects of Company Culture." *Harvard Business Review*. 29 Mar 2018.

[42] Church, Alan H. and Conger, Jay A. "When You Start a New Job, Pay Attention to These 5 Aspects of Company Culture." *Harvard Business Review*. 29 Mar 2018.

[43] https://www.amazon.jobs/principles.

[44] Church, Alan H. and Conger, Jay A. "When You Start a New Job, Pay Attention to These 5 Aspects of Company Culture." *Harvard Business Review*. 29 Mar 2018.

[45] Church, Alan H. and Conger, Jay A. "When You Start a New Job, Pay Attention to These 5 Aspects of Company Culture." *Harvard Business Review*. 29 Mar 2018.

[46] Church, Alan H. and Conger, Jay A. "When You Start a New Job, Pay Attention to These 5 Aspects of Company Culture." *Harvard Business Review*. 29 Mar 2018.

[47] Doyle, Alison. "Understanding Company Culture." *www.TheBalanceCareer.com*. 23 Aug 2018.

[48] Sixt, Kasey. Vice President, CKR Interactive, recruitment marketing and employee communications firm. Campbell, CA. *Interview 8 Aug 2018*.

[49] https://www.amazon.jobs/principles

[50] Lundrum, Sarah. "The Importance of Working for a Boss That Supports You." *Forbes*. 8 Dec 2017.

[51] Lundrum, Sarah. "The Importance of Working for a Boss That Supports You." *Forbes*. 8 Dec 2017.

[52] Mcleod, Lea. "8 Questions You Should Be Asking Your Boss." *TheMuse.com/advice*.

[53] Rossheim, John. "10 Ways Admins Can Make the Boss Look Good." *Monster.com-career advice*. 2018.

54 Rossheim, John. "10 Ways Admins Can Make the Boss Look Good." *Monster.com-career advice*. 2018.

55 "Why You Should Make Your Boss Look Good." Northwest Contract Services admins. Auburn, Washington. 24 May 2014.

56 Rossheim, John. "10 Ways Admins Can Make the Boss Look Good." *Monster.com-career advice*. 2018.

57 Kleiman, Jessica. "5 Ways to Make Your Boss Look Great—and Get Ahead in the Process." *TheMuse.com/advice*.

58 Sixt, Kasey. Vice President, CKR Interactive, recruitment marketing and employee communications firm. Campbell, CA. *Interview 8 Aug 2018*.

59 Kleiman, Jessica. "5 Ways to Make Your Boss Look Great—and Get Ahead in the Process." *TheMuse.com/advice*.

60 Winter, Jennifer. "How to Unlock the Hidden Secrets of Your Office." *TheMuse.com/advice*.

61 Winter, Jennifer. "How to Unlock the Hidden Secrets of Your Office." *TheMuse.com/advice*.

62 "How Well Are You Listening?" Elizabeth Bernstein. *The Wall Street Journal*. 13 Jan 2015.

63 www.Toastmasters.org/about/who-we-are.

64 Shewan, Dan. "16 Easy Ways to Improve Your Writing Skills." *The Word Stream Blog*. 2 Sept 2018.

65 https://www.amazon.jobs/principles

66 Premack, Rachel. "Jeff Bezos runs Amazon with 14 defined leadership principles. Here's how a 23-year-old engineer leveraged 5 of them to land a job." *Business Insider*. 4 Sept 2018.

67 https://www.amazon.jobs/principles

68 Premack, Rachel. "Jeff Bezos runs Amazon with 14 defined leadership principles. Here's how a 23-year-old engineer leveraged 5 of them to land a job." *Business Insider*. 4 Sept 2018.

69 Brefi Group. "Decision Making Skills." www.brefigroup.co.uk/training/decision_making.html.

[70] Lombardo, Jennifer. "Interpersonal Skills." http//study.com/academy/lessons.

[71] "Interpersonal skills." *www.SkillsYouNeed.com/interpersonal-skills.*

[72] "Why Does Diversity Matter?" *www.rbc.com.*

[73] Vasquez, Tina. "Andrés Tapia: Elevating a Buzzword." *Hispanic Executive.* 10 Dec 2015.

[74] Shontell, Alyson. "Steve Jobs Interviewed 20 People to be CEO of Apple and Disliked them All..." *Business Insider.* 15 Aug 2017.

[75] Cotteleer, Mark and Sniderman, Brenna. "Forces of change: Industry 4.0." *Deloitte Insights.* 18 Dec 2017.

[76] *Deloitte 2018 Millennial Survey.* Deloitte Touche Tohmatsu Limited (DTTL). March 2018.

[77] Okuszka, Jimmy. "4 Myths About Mentorship You Need to Stop Believing (if You Want to Get Ahead." *www.TheMuse.com/advice.*

[78] Okuszka, Jimmy. "4 Myths About Mentorship You Need to Stop Believing (if You Want to Get Ahead."/Alex Osten. *www.TheMuse.com/advice.*

[79] Okuszka, Jimmy. "4 Myths About Mentorship You Need to Stop Believing (if You Want to Get Ahead."/Daniel Zana. *www.TheMuse.com/advice.*

[80] Lewis, Jone Johnson. "How to Attract and Keep a Sponsor in Your Workplace." *TheBalanceCareer.com/*Training Tips. 25 Aug 2018.

[81] Driver, Saige. "Should You Hire a Career Coach?" *Business News Daily.* 21 June 2018.

[82] Cheeks, Demetrius. "10 Things You Should Know About Career Coaching." *Forbes.* 9 Jul 2013.

[83] Cheeks, Demetrius. "10 Things You Should Know About Career Coaching." *Forbes.* 9 Jul 2013.

[84] Cheeks, Demetrius. "10 Things You Should Know About Career Coaching." *Forbes.* 9 Jul 2013.

[85] **Carnegie,** Dale. *How to Win Friends and Influence People* (Gallery: New York, 1998) 52.

[86] Schafer, Jack. "Get Anyone to Like You—Instantly—Guaranteed!" *Psychology Today*. 30 Jul 2011.

[87] Carnegie, Dale. *How to Win Friends and Influence People* (Gallery: New York, 1998) 73.

[88] Bayer, Drake. "Four Tricks for Remembering Anybody's Name." *Fast Company*. 9 Apr 2013.

[89] Sixt, Kasey. Vice President, CKR Interactive, recruitment marketing and employee communications firm. Campbell, CA. Interview 8 Aug 2018.

[90] Frost, Aja. "10 Instant Ways to Be More Likeable." *TheMuse.com/Advice*.

[91] Dalton, Steve. "Harness the Ben Franklin Effect, Boost Your Career." *Huffpost*. 17 Jan 2014.

[92] Murphy, Jr., Bill. "19 Words That Will Make People Like You More" *Inc*. 13 May 2014.

[93] Rubin, Gretchen. "Eight Tips to Make Yourself More Likable and Win More Friends." *Slate.com*. 8 Apr 2009.

[94] https://www.amazon.jobs/principles

[95] Premack, Rachel. "Jeff Bezos runs Amazon with 14 defined leadership principles. Here's how a 23-year-old engineer leveraged 5 of them to land a job." *Business Insider*. 4 Sept 2018.

[96] Sixt, Kasey. Vice President, CKR Interactive, recruitment marketing and employee communications firm. Campbell, CA. Interview 8 Aug 2018.

[97] Shontell, Alyson. "Steve Jobs Interviewed 20 People to be CEO of Apple and Disliked them All..." *Business Insider*. 15 Aug 2017.

[98] Sixt, Kasey. Vice President, CKR Interactive, recruitment marketing and employee communications firm. Campbell, CA. Interview 8 Aug 2018.

[99] Casciaro, Tiziana, Gino, Francesca and Kouchaki, Maryam. "Learn to Love Networking." *Harvard Business Review*, 104-107. May 2016.

[100] Parikh, Jordan. "Why Professional Networking is So Important." *LinkedIn/Pulse*. 7 Nov 2016.

[101] Casciaro, Tiziana, Gino, Francesca and Kouchaki, Maryam. "Learn to Love Networking." *Harvard Business Review,* 104-107. May 2016.

[102] Prince, Russ Allen. "You Need Two Types of Professional Networks to Get Super-Rich." *Forbes.* 27 Oct 2017.

[103] Prince, Russ Allen. "You Need Two Types of Professional Networks to Get Super-Rich." *Forbes.* 27 Oct 2017.

[104] Bibby, Adrianne. "5 Types of Professional Networks and How to Use Them." *FlexJobs.com.* 19 Jan 2018.

[105] Bibby, Adrianne. "5 Types of Professional Networks and How to Use Them." *FlexJobs.com.* 19 Jan 2018.

[106] Bibby, Adrianne. "5 Types of Professional Networks and How to Use Them." *FlexJobs.com.* 19 Jan 2018.

[107] Casciaro, Tiziana, Gino, Francesca and Kouchaki, Maryam. "Learn to Love Networking." *Harvard Business Review,* 104-107. May 2016.

[108] Parikh, Jordan. "Why Professional Networking is So Important." *LinkedIn/Pulse.* 7 Nov 2016.

[109] Parikh, Jordan. "Why Professional Networking is So Important." *LinkedIn/Pulse.* 7 Nov 2016.

[110] Casciaro, Tiziana, Gino, Francesca and Kouchaki, Maryam. "Learn to Love Networking." *Harvard Business Review,* 104-107. May 2016.

[111] Sixt, Kasey. Vice President, CKR Interactive, recruitment marketing and employee communications firm. Campbell, CA. *Interview 8 Aug 2018.*

[112] Arruda, William. "Ten Ways to Build and Maintain your Professional Network." *www.ReachCC.com.* Reach Communications, 2009.

[113] Parikh, Jordan. "Why Professional Networking is So Important." *LinkedIn/Pulse.* 7 Nov 2016.

[114] Parikh, Jordan. "Why Professional Networking is So Important." *LinkedIn/Pulse.* 7 Nov 2016.

[115] Schwabel, Dan. "Why Face-to-Face Networking Still Trumps Social Networking." *Time Magazine.* 27 April 2012.

[116] Marcus, Bonnie. "The Networking Advice No One Tells You." *Forbes.* 22 May 2018.

[117] Marcus, Bonnie. "The Networking Advice No One Tells You." *Forbes.* 22 May 2018.

[118] Taylor, André interview. *www.AndreTaylor.com* 28 Aug 2018.

[119] Uzzi, Brian and Dunlop, Sharon. "How to Build Your Network." *Harvard Business Review.* Dec 2005.

[120] Casciaro, Tiziana, Gino, Francesca and Kouchaki, Maryam. "Learn to Love Networking." *Harvard Business Review,* 104-107. May 2016.

[121] Casciaro, Tiziana, Gino, Francesca and Kouchaki, Maryam. "Learn to Love Networking." *Harvard Business Review,* 104-107. May 2016.

[122] Cohen, Allen R. and Bradford, David L. *Influence Without Authority.* Hoboken, NJ: Wiley, 2005.

[123] Casciaro, Tiziana, Gino, Francesca and Kouchaki, Maryam. "Learn to Love Networking." *Harvard Business Review,* 104-107. May 2016.

[124] Moore, Susie. "Six Best Podcasts You're Going to Love Listening To." *www.TheMuse.com/Advice.* 2019.

###

www.ingramcontent.com/pod-product-compliance
Lightning Source LLC
Chambersburg PA
CBHW020635220526
45464CB00001B/152